REMOTE CONTROL CHILDHOOD?

Combating the Hazards of Media Culture

Diane E. Levin

National Association for the Education of Young Children
1509 16th Street, NW
Washington, D.C.

**National Association for the Education of Young Children
1509 16th Street, NW
Washington, DC 20036-1426
800-424-2460 or 202-232-8777
Website: http://www.naeyc.org**

The National Association for the Education of Young Children (NAEYC) attempts through its publications program to provide a forum for discussion of major issues and ideas in our field. We hope to provoke thought and promote professional growth. The views expressed or implied are not necessarily those of the Association. NAEYC wishes to thank the author, who donated much time and effort to develop this book as a contribution to our profession.

Library of Congress Catalog Number: 97-80647

ISBN: 0-935989-84-6

NAEYC #326

Editor: Carol Copple; *Design and production:* Jack Zibulsky and Sandi Collins; *Copyeditor:* Sandi Collins; *Front cover photo:* Robert Kyle.

Printed in the United States of America

CONTENTS

LIST OF TABLES AND FIGURES

ACKNOWLEDGMENTS

First and foremost, I want to thank Gary Goldstein and Eli Levin-Goldstein, who have taught me so much about what it means to work together as a family to tame the media in our lives. Second, my deepest thanks and appreciation go to Nancy Carlsson-Paige, with whom I have come to understand the power of media, media violence, and media culture in children's lives as well as to savor the strength that comes from working collaboratively to change it.

This book would not be what it is without the unique contributions of Lori Pino and Christine Gerzon, former students and current colleagues, devoted teachers of young children, who have helped develop and try out many of the activities described in this book. They have taught me so much. My special thanks and admiration go to them.

To Molly Fontaine, Chris Giguere, Chris Morton, Kathy Roberts, Honey Schnapp, and Heidi White, Boston area members of TRUCE (Teachers for Resisting Unhealthy Children's Entertainment), who have contributed to the spirit and substance of this book in more ways than I can list here. Thank you. I hope TRUCE continues for many years to come.

To my dear friends in New Zealand (especially Marilyn Head and members of Play for Life) who have taught me so much about how to take action on children's behalf—thank you for helping me believe that when we all work together to resist the hazards of media culture, we can make a lasting difference.

To Wheelock colleagues, Gail Dines and Petra Hesse, with whom I have developed and taught the annual summer institute, Media Education in a Violent Society, and a media literacy specialty in the graduate school—thank you. Our work together has helped me better understand how powerful a multifaceted approach to dealing with the hazards of media culture can be.

To the many teachers and parents whose stories about their efforts with children have contributed so much to the substance of this book. Special thanks go to Connie Biewald, Jane Davidson, Karen Economopoulos, Betty Jane Adams, Sarah Napier, and Debbie Rollins.

To colleagues and friends who are working around the United States to counteract the negative impact of media and the media culture on children and to create a healthier environment in which children can develop and grow. Thanks especially to Blakely Bundy, Barbara Hildt, Susan Hopkins, Bonita Klemm, Chris Lamm, Peggy Schirmer, Jacqueline Sears, Craig

Simpson, Sunny Wallick, and Daphne White. Your energy, commitment, and insights helped motivate me to undertake the project of writing this book.

My special thanks and appreciation go to Zell Draz for her continuing belief in and generous support of this work.

To Wheelock College, thank you for understanding my need to keep the many facets of my professional life—teaching, scholarship, advocacy, and activism—healthy and strong.

My thanks and appreciation go to Carol Copple, NAEYC editor par excellence, whose gentle prodding and insightful guidance helped me make this a much more comprehensive and coherent book than it otherwise would have been. Thanks too, to Sandi Collins, whom I could always count on for clear communication and skillful copyediting.

And finally, to NAEYC, thank you for your continuing commitment to finding effective and innovative ways to best serve the interests of children, parents, and teachers.

Carolyn Boriss-Krimsky helped create the media monster collage on page viii; Lori Pino of Cotuit-Marstons Mills Elementary School, Barnstable, Massachusetts, contributed the dialogue on pages 25–26, the questionnaire on page 47, the children's TV-viewing rules on pages 68–69, the letters on pages 113–14, and the classroom account on pages 98–101; Nancy Carlsson-Paige helped with the letter on page 49; Chris Morton and members of Youth Enlightening Youth, Newburyport, Massachusetts, contributed the letter on page 50; Connie Biewald and Sarah Napier of Fayerweather Street School, Cambridge, Massachusetts, supplied the account on page 56 and the guide on page 112; Jane Davidson at the University of Delaware Laboratory School shared the classroom activity on pages 59–60; Christine Gerzan shared the mouse family activity on pages 73–74 and the account on page 105; Gretchen West contributed the scenario on page 79; Debbie Rollins shared the dramatic-play account on pages 81–82; Honey Schnapp helped develop the toy selection guide on page 83; Karen Economopoulos shared the letter on pages 92–93; Betty Jane Adams of the Washington Early Childhood Learning Center, Kingsport, Tennessee, wrote the scenario on pages 103–04; Dolores Hermann and the Dearhaven Child Care and Learning Center, Lake Forest, Illinois, contributed the letter on pages 122–23; Blakely Fetridge Bundy, director of the Winnetka (Illionois) Alliance for Early Childhood, shared the ideas on pages 150–51; the Campaign Against Toys of Violence Steering Committee of the Cambridge Peace Commission distributed the flyer on page 152; and Bonita Klemm contributed the letter on page 155.

The Media Monster (or, Is TV Too Violent?)

Kids are constantly bombarded by cartoons with big strong characters that always fight and never get hurt. I don't think that getting shot with a gun wouldn't even leave a mark on your body. If a 300-pound boulder fell on your head, would you get up?

Children's TV shows us that violence is a natural and normal way to solve problems. Watching people fight without hurting each other makes us think that violence has no consequences. It is a cycle that never gets broken.

From when we are 3 years old until about 10, all we see on TV is violent cartoons. When we get older, we see violent horror and action films. As adults we watch the news with all the violent robberies, rapes, and murders while we are eating dinner with our families. Eventually, we become so immune to violence that we are not even surprised or horrified when we see or hear about any violence in the world.

TV can be like a monster manipulating our thoughts, feelings, and emotions.

—Eli Levin-Goldstein
Creator of the Media Monster shown above

It Takes a Village to Protect Children Growing Up in the Media Culture

Soon after my son Eli entered kindergarten, he was invited to a birthday party for one of his new school friends. Calvin was a first grader in a combined-grade classroom. I was a bit anxious because I had met Calvin's parents only once. Eli and I went shopping to buy a gift. After much discussion about what Calvin might like, Eli decided on a fancy box of "smelling" magic markers (each color with a different smell) and a sketch pad.

When we arrived at the party, Eli happily ran off, and after a brief chat with Calvin's parents, I left. When I returned at pickup time, Eli came bouncing up to me and enthusiastically asked me to "Come see Calvin's gifts." What I saw was a pile of action figures and other items that were all connected to a TV program or movie with fighting themes—Masters of the Universe, GI Joe, and Transformers were very popular at that time—and over to the side, the box of magic markers and sketch pad.

Trying to find a nonthreatening way to get a sense of Calvin's mother's reaction to the gifts, I casually said, "It looks like Calvin got an arsenal for his birthday." She shrugged, then said, "We didn't allow any war toys into the house until Calvin's birthday party last year after he entered kindergarten. Most of the kids brought presents like this. I couldn't send them all back, so after that we had to change our approach. Then Calvin began nagging to see the TV shows that went with the toys, which he had only watched at other houses until then."

The ever-expanding media culture

As Eli and I left the party and got into the car, I knew that the media culture had entered our lives in a new way. The next time Eli was invited to a birthday party, there would be a lot more stress over what gift to buy. And I also suspected that the equilibrium we previously had reached over Eli's own media-linked toys with fighting themes would soon need to be renegotiated. I was right on both counts.

About a month later, Eli was at another birthday party for a new school friend. When I went to pick him up, I found all the children huddled in a little room watching a video of the movie *Raiders of the Lost Ark*. It is a movie I would not have chosen for Eli to see at his level of development and experience because it contains content that is scary and violent and cannot possibly be understood by 5- and 6-year-olds. Once again, media culture had entered Eli's life in a way over which I had no control.

The next school year began with the Teenage Mutant Ninja Turtles being a major presence in the play culture of Eli and his friends. The TV show and its spin-off toys were enormously popular. Then, the night before the movie was due to open, Eli received a call from the class Turtle expert inviting him to go to the opening after school on Friday. Eli was thrilled to have been chosen. Fortunately, I thought, we were going out of town after school that day, so to Eli's great unhappiness, we had to turn down the invitation. But on Monday morning when Eli realized that he was the only boy in his classroom who had not seen the movie, I knew the issue was far from over.

A couple of years later, we were on an airplane and the inflight movie had a rape scene that showed all but the actual sex act. My son saw his first rape. When I voiced concern to the flight attendant about the inappropriateness of the movie for children and asked how I could lodge a complaint, several other parents, who had overheard, expressed their appreciation to me.

Soon after the airplane episode, Mike Tyson went on trial for rape. The trial coverage was everywhere in the news. While we rarely watched the news at our house when Eli was around, he arrived home from school one day to ask what rape was and whether I had heard about Tyson.

I could go on and on describing how, as a parent, I have watched media and the media culture enter my son's life in ways in which I had little or no control, and I have watched media play an increasingly central role in his life (he is now 15). Throughout, I have tried to create a home in which television, videos, movies, and other media are consumed responsibly and thoughtfully—where the positive aspects of media and media culture can rise to the top and where there is a balance between my own adult sense of what is appropriate and Eli's interests, desires, and experiences. Most of the time I feel as if I'm holding my finger in a dike; even though water keeps trickling in, I need to keep my finger there to prevent the water from pouring in and causing a flood.

When it comes to dealing with media and media culture in children's lives, we all have varying degrees of knowledge, skill, and resources. Many parents struggle to take care of their children's basic needs and do not have the resources I did to try to keep my finger in the dike. Still, I have rarely worked with a parent who has not talked about trying in some way to deal with the media and media culture in their children's lives. Most families, like my own, deal with these issues in isolation, with few existing supports for parents, among themselves, in schools, or in the wider community. My son's school certainly did not see dealing with the media in children's lives as a major role or responsibility of the school[1]—nor do most schools I visit. In fact, few schools in the United States see this as their responsibility.

Needed: A community of support

My experiences parenting in media culture would have been a lot easier and more effective if parents and teachers in my son's school community had worked together to support each other in their efforts to deal effectively with family media issues, concerns, and struggles. Then, for instance, there would have been an avenue for discussing the movies my son saw at friends' homes.

It would have helped even more if parents, schools, and communities all over the country had been doing the same thing. Then I might not have been the first parent to stand up and complain when an airplane movie showed a rape scene when many children were on board. And the airline might have gotten a deluge of complaints from parents and had to take seriously the needs of the children on board when making choices about what movies to show. It would have felt as if I had a whole village helping me counteract the problems created by the media for my child. Everyone in the village would have been working together for the good of all children.

I hope this book will help to create that village, that it will contribute to the groundswell of activism and collaboration needed to create a more positive media culture for children. When my son was young, my husband and I always thought we should be able to deal effectively with the media on our own. We quickly figured out that we were in over our heads. The remote control of the media often undermined our direct control as parents. There was not much out there to help us in our efforts.

Then, fortunately, in March of 1995, I went to New Zealand to work with a group of parents and educators who had formed a group called Play for Life. The media and media culture created in the United States are heavily exported to countries around the world, and the children of New Zealand are not exempt. Play for Life was founded to counteract the negative effects of media and media culture on children and to promote healthy play. It strives to educate the public about the forces undermining healthy play and works to create an environment that better nurtures play.

The small group of highly committed individuals in Play for Life has been an effective force in New Zealand. Its efforts succeeded in getting the Children's Television Code, creating a mechanism for citizens to have a voice in the media that get aired for children in New Zealand. It also succeeded in using the code to get *The Mighty Morphin Power Rangers* taken off the air because the program was found to violate the code provision that places limitations on showing gratuitous acts of violence to children. In addition, as a result of the ruling, many toy stores refused to carry Power Ranger toys. At the time of my visit, members of Play for Life were working to expand their efforts to bring their concerns about media and media culture to parents, teachers, government officials, media representatives, and toy producers.

The month I spent in New Zealand with Play for Life showed me just how much the voice of one small group of committed individuals can make a difference in the world we create for children. The members helped me see that creating a village is possible. I realized that what works in one country will not necessarily translate directly to another country. Nonetheless, I came home energized to find others who wanted to work to create a healthier media environment for children here in the United States.

A short time after my return from New Zealand the opportunity arose to act on this goal. I spoke about the Mighty Morphin Power Rangers at a child care directors' meeting organized by the Boston Association for the Education of Young Children (BAEYC). The meeting, which usually had about 15 attendees, attracted approximately 50 directors. We talked about the problems the Power Rangers were creating for children and teachers at child care centers and discussed possible effective responses.

I ended my talk by announcing that a Power Ranger movie was scheduled to open at theaters that summer. After a pause, someone said, "We can't just sit back. We have to do something!" Others nodded. I offered to work with them if they decided to organize "something."

The next week I got a call from Chris Giguere, a BAEYC board member who had volunteered to take on the task of getting things going. With the support of BAEYC and other organizations, we founded Teachers for Resisting Unhealthy Children's Entertainment (TRUCE). As our first activity, we organized the Teachers Campaign Against the Power Rangers Movie, which involved preparing and distributing materials about the movie to child care centers around the country. Our goal was to get the centers to copy and distribute materials as widely as possible. We included action ideas for parents, schools, and the wider community so everyone could find something to do.

After that initial campaign, TRUCE continued to use the same approach to develop other educational campaigns on media and children's issues. Then, in the summer of 1996, as part of the Massachusetts Medical Society's effort to develop a public health campaign on media violence, I worked with TRUCE members to write the booklet the medical society published, *Help Children See Through Violence in the Media*. The response to the booklet was immediate—it helped teachers and parents feel like they could do something about media and media violence issues and helped them get started. People all over the country made copies to distribute in their communities. That booklet formed the basis for this book.

Help Children See Through Violence in the Media proved to me that many people around the country are ready to work toward creating a village to protect children from the harmful aspects of media, media violence, and media culture. This recognition provided the motivation and discipline I needed to write this book. I hope that in the midst of much of the depressing information that this book contains, you will see it as the cause for optimism that I do.

Creating a village that supports the development of more positive media and media culture for children will require efforts at all levels of society— with children and adults in homes, schools, and communities, and with policymakers, TV stations, and the media industry.

I hope you will use this book to help you act and to mobilize others. A little bit of action from each of us along the lines of the activities suggested in this book will go a long way toward convincing the media and toy industries, and government officials and policymakers as well, that it is in their own self-interest to stop marketing violence and other harmful lessons to our children.

At the same time, children still will face the current realities of their remote control childhoods; so as we work to change how things are, we also will need to find ways to reduce the power and the negative impact of media culture on children. Perhaps this book will help you work with children on issues of media violence as you also work to create the remedies.

How this book is organized

Remote Control Childhood? is divided into three parts. Part 1 focuses on background information to expand your understanding of media, media violence, and the media culture and how it affects children. Part 2 provides information about developing strategies for working effectively with children in classrooms on the full range of ways media, media violence, and media culture touch children's lives. Part 3 focuses on strategies for working on media issues outside the classroom, with parents, in schools, and in the wider community.

Throughout this book, you will find information that explains the important issues underlying each topic. You also will find guidelines to help you clarify how to work on these issues, action ideas that provide concrete suggestions for how you might begin, and numerous examples that illustrate how teachers, parents, and others working on these issues in the wider community have translated the suggestions into practice in their particular settings.

What you will not find are simple prescriptions about what to do to make it all better. Complex problems require complex solutions; the more you can shape your use of the contents of this book to fit your situation, the more effective and meaningful your efforts will be. Use this book in a way that works for you. Start small, see how things go, adapt strategies, build onto them. Share your efforts and successes with others. Find whatever ways you can—however big or small—to help create the village that will protect children from the dangers of a remote control childhood.

Because *Remote Control Childhood?* is written for teachers and parents, some chapters are directed more at one group than the other. One approach for using this book is to read and use those parts of the book that are most relevant for your situation and needs. But if you read all the chapters, you will discover strategies that can be adapted to both home and school and that can help parents and teachers better understand each other's point of view.

ESTABLISHING A FOUNDATION

PART

1

What's the Problem with Media Culture and Media Violence?

Ever since television became a daily staple of American family life, its influence on children has been the subject of study and debate. No aspect of the debate has been more heated than violence in the media—how it affects children and how it contributes to their developing ideas about violence, their aggressive behavior, and whom they grow up to become as adults. In this decade, with the entrance of video and computer games and now the Internet, children can interact directly with increasingly realistic and graphic violence.

In recent years the level of violence in U.S. society and in the media has become of increasing concern. We also have learned a lot more about the influence of media and media violence on violent behavior and other aspects of development and learning. This growing knowledge base has shifted the focus of the debate from whether media violence contributes to violence in real life to what can be done to deal with and reduce the violence.

Children growing up today spend an enormous amount of time glued to the TV screen. They average 35 hours per week of screen time, either watching TV or playing video games. Before entering kindergarten they are likely to have spent 4,000 hours watching television—more time than they spent doing anything but sleeping, more time even than they will spend in school.

Both the quantity and quality of violence children see on the screen have increased dramatically in the past decade. By the end of elementary school the average child will have witnessed 8,000 murders and 100,000 other acts of violence on the TV screen. Most of that violence is on programs that have entertainment or "for fun" violence—on cartoon and drama programs created to "entertain"—and is perpetrated by characters who have "good qualities that make them attractive role models to viewers." The National Television Violence Study points out that glamorized violence "is of particular concern for younger children, who often lack the capability to link outcomes and punishments shown later in a program to earlier violent acts."[2]

Violence is also on the rise in other media targeted toward children, especially in computer and video games. In a recent survey, 93% of boys and 78% of girls reported playing video games.[3] And 25% of those surveyed said they played video games between two and three hours a day. The video-game industry had retail sales of almost $4 billion in 1996. Well over 50% of video games are violent, and the violence is increasingly graphic and realistic. Because video games not only show violence but also make the players the perpetrators of the violent acts, their negative impact on children can be greater than the impact of merely viewing violence on the screen.[4] Increasingly, children also see and interact with violence on the Internet—3.3 million households had access by 1996 and that figure is growing fast.

In addition to the entertainment violence, children hear about and see real-world violence on TV news. More than two-thirds of U.S. households have the television on at dinner when news programs report the gory details of the day's real-world violence. And while children cannot fully differentiate between what on the screen is pretend and what is real, they do get input about an endless variety of violent ways people treat each other.

Deregulation of children's television

Much of the escalating concern about how media and violence in the media affect children can be traced back to deregulation of children's television in 1984 by the Federal Communications Commission. With deregulation it became possible for the first time to market toys and other products with TV programs. Within one year of deregulation, 9 of the 10 best-selling toys were connected to TV shows, and 7 of those shows were violent. The sale of toys of violence, including action figures with weapons, soared more than 600% in three years.[5]

After deregulation, one TV show after another became the craze—*Masters of the Universe, GI Joe, Teenage Mutant Ninja Turtles, The Mighty Morphin Power Rangers.* Each successive show was more violent than the one before—each Power Rangers episode averages about 100 acts of violence, twice as many as the *Teenage Mutant Ninja Turtles,* the previously most successful show.

Furthermore, each successive popular show, made for the explicit purpose of selling toys and other products, sold more products. At its peak the Ninja Turtles industry claimed to have more than 1,000 products on store shelves. In 1994 the Mighty Morphin Power Rangers reached a landmark; retail sales of its toys and other products surpassed $1 billion. And in 1996, even before the re-release of the movie trilogy, Star Wars action figures were the best-selling toy after Barbie, and all-time sales for Star Wars merchandise had reached $4 billion.

Below is a list of the most popular children's programs on TV in 1995 (the most recent figures available). Each of these programs focused on violence and contained scary content. Each show also produced entire lines of toys and other licensed products.

Most Popular Children's TV Shows in 1995

1. Goosebumps

2. Spider-Man

3. Mighty Morphin Power Rangers

4. Masked Rider

5. X-Men

Source: G. Fabrikant, "The Young and Restless Audience," *The New York Times*, 18 April 1996, pp. D1, D8.

ACTION IDEA

Use this chart (as well as others throughout this book) as a tool to involve others in efforts to reduce media violence and its effects on children. Copy and distribute the information to others. Add new and updated facts you hear about or read in the news.

It is unlikely that any of the shows listed above would have been made without the deregulation of television; they were produced to sell merchandise, and only deregulation made that possible. This new marketing strategy creates a dramatic and worrisome change in the social and play environment of young children. Many of the most popular shows are violent, so when children play, the highly realistic toys that are linked to their favorite shows keep them focused on imitating the violence they see on the screen. More and more of children's playtime is taken up imitating violent TV themes.

Now, as this book goes to press, we are seeing the carefully orchestrated buildup of the most violent and sexualized media phenomenon marketed to children (and adults) so far—Spawn. Based on the best-selling comic-book series, a 1997 movie, and a new TV show, Spawn action figures are on toy shelves. Female Spawn characters have highly exaggerated gender characteristics, carry many weapons, and are scantily clad in bizarre outfits, including a brassiere made of skulls.[6] (See Chapter 6 for photographs of Spawn figures from toy boxes.) Spawn figures were on the toy industry's list of successful toys introduced in 1996. For many elementary-school boys, they are the "cool" toy to have. And the toy's box indicates that the figures are "for ages 4 and up."

And with the premiere of *Starship Troopers* in November 1997, we see the link-up of a highly violent and sexualized R-rated movie with a line of toys marketed to children ages 5 and up. Now a TV program is being considered.[7]

The violent themes of many video games, coupled with their increasing linkage to popular TV shows and toy lines, further involve children with violence. It was not long after deregulation that the phenomenon of remote control childhood gained momentum. Video-game systems and electronic games for home computers were introduced, quickly achieving enormous popularity. Video games can lure children into continued involvement in media violence long after they outgrow violent media-linked toys. In the elementary-school years video games often replace creative and complex play as the out-of-school activity of choice with and without peers.

The phenomenon of massive media cross-feeding is flourishing. TV shows, movies, video games, comic books, children's books, and, most recently, World Wide Web sites are all marketed together. Media cross-feeding creates an environment wherein children are deluged with media images that are hard to avoid and rapidly enter their childhood culture.

The table on page 13 shows some of the more salient facts and figures about media and media violence in children's lives. It illustrates the enormity of the role media, media violence, and related products play in children's lives.

Some Facts and Figures about Media, Media Violence, and Children

Children average 35 hours per week of *screen time,* which includes TV, movies, video and computer games, and videotapes.

By the time children enter kindergarten, they will have seen 4,000 hours of TV.

The average child sees 20,000 advertisements a year.

By the end of elementary school, children will have witnessed an average of 8,000 murders and 100,000 other violent acts.

Children's cartoon/action programs average more than 20 acts of violence per hour, compared with 5 acts of violence per hour during prime-time television.

Half of U.S. households with children aged 6–14 years have video-game systems—and a majority of video games contain violent images.

Half of the toys sold in 1994 were linked to movies or TV programs (up from 10% in 1984).

Sales of the following products each reached approximately $1 billion in 1994:

• products with Mighty Morphin Power Ranger logo

• TV-linked action figure toys (most were violent)

• children's home videos

• children's books (most best-sellers were linked to TV programs)

As of January 1997 (before the re-release of the *Star Wars* trilogy), $4 billion of Star Wars products had been sold, and the figure was rising rapidly.

Source: American Psychological Association, *Violence and Youth: Psychology's Response, Volume 1, Summary Report* (Washington, DC: Author, 1993); D. Walsh, *Selling Out America's Children: How America Puts Profits Before Values—And What Parents Can Do* (Minneapolis: Fairview, 1994); and others (see Note 8).

What the research says

Research can help us understand the effects of many aspects of media on children. On the one hand, some studies look at programs, such as *Mister Rogers' Neighborhood,* designed to educate in developmentally appropriate ways as well as to entertain. One such study found that *Mister Rogers' Neighborhood* promotes positive social behavior in children.[9]

On the other hand, a rapidly growing body of research shows how violence in the media harms children and contributes to the epidemic of violence we are now seeing among our youth. Most experts agree that media violence has harmful effects on children's development and behavior.[10] The following chart summarizes key areas of concern.

The Effects of Media Violence on Children

Media violence

- causes an increase in mean-spirited, aggressive behavior[11]

- causes increased levels of fearfulness, mistrust, and self-protective behavior toward others[12]

- contributes to desensitization and callousness to the effects of violence and the suffering of others

- provides violent heroes whom children seek to emulate

- provides justification for resorting to violence when children think they are right

- creates an increasing appetite for viewing more violence and more extreme violence

- fosters a culture in which disrespectful behavior becomes a legitimate way for people to treat each other

Source: American Medical Association, *Physician Guide to Media Violence* (Chicago: Author 1996).

Teachers voice concern

These research findings reflect what many teachers have been saying for a long time about how media violence affects the children in their classrooms. For example, one study found that more than 90% of teachers believed the Mighty Morphin Power Rangers contributed to violent behavior—in play and in how children handled conflicts.[13] Many teachers say they are spending more and more of their classroom time trying to deal with aggressive and unfocused behavior of more and more children. Conflict-resolution and violence-prevention programs are springing up all over the country, initially for middle- and high-school students, increasingly now for elementary and even preschool children. When asked, teachers increasingly connect violence in the media to the problems they see.

Teachers also point to concerns over the nature of the play in their classrooms.[14] Many children seem to use playtime to imitate the violence they see on the screen rather than to develop creative, imaginative play of their own making. In addition, these children often impose this violent content and behavior on the play of others. In such a situation the quality of play (and therefore, learning) is undermined for all children in early childhood classrooms.

There's more to media violence than fists and fights

When people talk about media violence they usually are referring to screen action in which someone physically hurts or tries to hurt someone else. But from a child's point of view, violence goes far beyond the infliction of physical harm.

Young children experience violence whenever they feel endangered and unsafe—by things that undermine the sense of safety of their thoughts, feelings, bodies, or who they are. Demeaning language (such as "put-downs"), gender and racial stereotypes, abuse of power (for instance, when one group exploits another), and deviousness (for example, when advertisers mislead children) can undermine a child's sense that the world is a safe and just place. This content also contributes to what children learn about violence and about how people function in their world.

To deal fully with the issues of media violence in children's lives, we need to define violence broadly and look at the whole range of ways it undermines children's sense of safety and enters into the meanings children make of their world. We need to look at how violence is a part of the overall "culture of disrespect"[15] that surrounds children in the media and popular culture.

Beyond violence: The media culture

While much of the public debate about media and children has focused on violence on the screen, today's children are growing up in a media culture that permeates most of their lives.[16] For instance, media affect children's ideas about such things as the toys they want to play with and the content of their play; what they want to eat and wear and how they want to look; what it means to be a child and a grown-up and the nature of the relationships between them; what it means to be male and female and the nature of gender relationships; and what it means to be rich and poor and the role played by consumerism.

Much of what media culture teaches children is not what the adults who care about them would choose for them to learn. It also is not what child development theory and research tell us is what children need. Here are but a few examples of how the media culture can negatively influence children's behavior and ideas:

- **Media can undermine children's willingness to look to the important adults in their lives for nurturance and support.** What children often see in the media, especially in children's programming, is a world in which "children know what's best." It is a world in which adults are nonexistent and children function fully on their own, where adults are inept fools constantly outsmarted by the children or where adults constantly create roadblocks to the things children really want. Could this be contributing to the phenomenon parents and teachers report about how their children are beginning to rebel against adult authority—starting their adolescent rebellions—at younger and younger ages?

- **Advertising and its emphasis on consuming more and more products create a culture that undermines many children's inner confidence and resourcefulness.** Children see thousands of advertisements that promise to bring them happiness if they only can have the particular toy (or breakfast cereal) being advertised. Then, after they get the item, children quickly find that the object does not live up to its promises, and they become bored.

  Seeing objects rather than themselves as the source of personal fulfillment and happiness prevents children from actively using their own resources to become engaged in the world in a meaningful and satisfying way. This helps explain why children often say they are bored in the midst of plenty and why many seem to have few inner resources to bring to their play and learning.

- **The media culture also provides children with many kinds of worrisome stereotypes about people—including race, class, and gender.** For instance, children regularly see unhealthily thin woman portrayed on the screen as admirable, glamorous, and desirable. Girls now go on diets at younger and younger ages, and eating disorders are on the rise among girls of all ages.

    Children also are exposed to more and increasingly graphic sexual imagery and behavior. Usually, sex is portrayed solely as a physical act out of the context of a loving relationship. It also is often linked to violence. This content cannot be fully understood by children (although they do try to figure it out), and it can blur the boundaries between childhood and adulthood. For example, there are beauty pageants in which young girls wear glamourous makeup and costumes and perform elaborate routines, as the American public became abruptly aware of when JonBenet Ramsey, a young pageant star, was murdered in 1996.

While there is far less research or discussion about the role of these broader media influences on children than about media violence, it is clear that the media culture in which today's children are growing up is a vastly different environment from the one in which the adults who care for them grew up. Media is a teacher that competes with us all for the hearts and minds of children. Any efforts to deal effectively with the media and media violence in children's lives must take into account the scope of media's influence and power. (See Appendix A, the NAEYC Position Statement on Media Violence in Children's Lives.)

Whose responsibility is it?

For far too long, much of the burden of dealing with the problems created for children by media, media violence, and media culture has been placed on parents. The media and toy industries (and many government officials, policy-makers, and even teachers) tell parents it is their job to limit their children's exposure to media violence. Similar arguments have begun to surface over children's access to violence, sex, and sites/ads on the World Wide Web.

But raising a "post-deregulation" child (born after 1984) presents difficult challenges that parents raising "pre-deregulation" children did not have to face. Because of the all-pervasiveness of media culture in everyday life, some parents now see media violence as normal, having become desensitized to the effects it may be having on their children. Many other parents who try to play an active role in limiting their children's exposure to media's negative aspects say their efforts often lead to many problems—for instance, never-ending struggles with their children. They also say that despite their best efforts, they still meet with only limited success as their children are exposed to media violence and violent media-linked toys elsewhere—at the homes of friends and relatives, shopping malls, video stores, and fast-food restaurants. This is a very different story than parents of pre-deregulation children generally tell.

To say it is parents' job alone to protect their children from media violence is nothing less than a cop-out. Furthermore, it is irresponsible and unfair. It makes one of the most important jobs in a society—raising children to become responsible and contributing members of society—more difficult for parents than it already is in these stressful times. The problems created by media, media violence, and media culture should not be left to parents to deal with on their own. And to place the whole burden on parents leaves the media and toy industries free to continue to rake in enormous profits from the violence and other aspects of media culture they market to children.

All of society is paying the price for the failure to protect children from remote control and to create a positive media environment that supports parents' efforts to raise healthy children. The lessons children learn from the culture of violence created by the media are played out every day in classrooms, school yards, homes, and the wider community.

Cause for hope

Media violence and other aspects of media culture are a public health issue that affects us all. Professionals trained to care about the well-being of children and society—among them the American Academy of Pediatrics, the American Medical Association, the American Psychological Association, the National Association for the Education of Young Children, the National Parent-Teachers Association, and the U.S. Surgeon General and Attorney General—have begun saying enough is enough.

In recent years the federal government has attempted to assert its role in protecting children from the excesses of the media industry that resulted in large part from deregulation.[17] The 1996 Telecommunications Act requires that, beginning in 1998, new TV sets will be equipped with the V-chip, a microchip device that allows parents to program their TV sets to let through only those shows they want their children to watch. Programming the V-chip requires a program ratings system—the nature of which is the subject of

Voice your opinions about the TV ratings system by contacting TV Parental Guidelines Monitoring Board, P.O. Box 14097, Washington, DC 20004; 202-879-9364; e-mail tvomb@usa.net.

heated debate. The exact nature of the ratings (how much information they should give) and who should develop them (independent groups and experts versus the media industry) have been the subject of much controversy.

In December 1996 the TV industry developed a voluntary program-ratings system—officially known as TV Parental Guidelines—modeled after the age-based movie ratings. When child advocates and parent and education groups wanted content designations added to the ratings, the industry agreed, and the amended system went into effect in October 1997 (only two networks refused to carry the ratings). The ratings that now appear on the TV screen are shown on page 20.

It was a major breakthrough that the television industry acknowledged, for the first time, that it has a role to play in helping parents and society deal with the problems media are creating for children. Whether or not the ratings system becomes the standard for V-chip programming, most experts see the V-chip as only a small piece of the solution to media violence anyhow.[18] Concern is also voiced about the fact that the V-chip continues to leave the sole burden of controlling media violence on parents. At the same time the V-chip and rating system provide parents with the possibility of a little bit more control over the media in their children's lives, and every little bit helps.

The Children's Television Act (CTA), passed in 1990 to require stations to meet the educational and informational needs of children as a condition for license renewal, proved ineffective. In 1996, after years of inaction on CTA's implementation, the Federal Communications Commission finally revised the rules, requiring TV stations to provide a weekly minimum of three hours of quality children's programming. But this rule revision does nothing to limit the amount of violence on children's TV programs or on programs aired during children's prime-time viewing hours. It also does nothing to reinstate the ban (which existed until 1984) against linking violent TV programs with violent toys, a pairing which can deeply influence the lessons children learn.

Still, the fact that we are again seeing the U.S. government assert its right and responsibility to create a healthier media culture for children and

Parental Guidelines Developed by the TV Industry

For children

TVY   **All Children.** Designed to be appropriate for all children, including children from ages 2–6. Whether animated or live action, the themes and elements in this program are not expected to frighten younger children.

TVY7   **Directed to Older Children.** Designed for children 7 years old and above, but perhaps more appropriate for children who have acquired the developmental skills needed to distinguish between make-believe and reality. May include mild fantasy violence or comedic violence that may frighten children under the age of 7; therefore, it may be unsuitable for very young children. Note: Those programs with more intense or combative fantasy violence will be designated TV-Y7-FV.

For the entire viewing audience

TVG   **General Audience.** Designed to be suitable for all ages. Parents may let most younger children watch this program unattended. It contains little or no violence, no strong language, and little or no sexual dialogue or situations.

TVPG **Parental Guidance Suggested.** Contains material that parents may find unsuitable for young children. Many parents may want to watch it with their younger children. The theme itself may call for parental guidance and/or the program may contain one or more of the following: moderate violence (V), some sexual situations (S), infrequent coarse language (L), or some suggestive dialogue (D).

TV14   **Parents Strongly Cautioned.** Contains some material that parents would find unsuitable for children under 14 years of age. Parents are strongly urged to exercise great care in monitoring and letting children under the age of 14 watch unattended. Contains one or more of the following: intense violence (V), intense sexual situations (S), strong coarse language (L), or intensely suggestive dialogue (D).

For adults only

TVMA **Mature Audience Only.** Specifically designed to be viewed by adults and therefore may be unsuitable for children under 17. Contains one or more of the following: graphic violence (V), explicit sexual activity (S), or crude, indecent language (L).

Sources: Motion Picture Association of America, National Association of Broadcasters, and National Cable Television Association. (See also Note 19.)

protect children from the worst abuses of the media industry is cause for growing optimism. It paves the way for the Federal Communications Commission to deal with other media and children's issues emerging with the new technologies, such as the material children have access to and the advertising directed to children on the Internet.[20]

Because media are and will continue to be a significant presence in children's lives, we must make media as positive a force in children's lives as we can. While this book generally focuses on how to deal with the problems created by media, it does provide information that can help parents and teachers make informed decisions about how to make media a positive contributor to children's lives.

And another positive trend—the growing effort to promote appropriate, quality media for children—will help us. More materials are being published, such as *The Kids First! Directory: A Consumer's Guide to Quality Children's Videos and CD-ROMS*,[21] that help parents and teachers make informed choices about the media they use with children. In 1994 the Public Broadcasting System launched its far-reaching Ready-to-Learn Service.[22] Through local public television affiliates, Ready-to-Learn provides training and resources on appropriate media and appropriate use of media to parents and child care providers in many communities throughout the United States.

Another positive trend is the increasing amount of media designed to promote positive development and learning in young children. In September 1997, commercial TV networks began introducing new programs developed specifically to meet the mandated three hours of quality programming for children.[23] And public television has introduced several new children's programs dealing with such issues as social development and appreciation of cultural diversity (*The Puzzle Place*) and early appreciation of books and reading (*Reading Time*).

A call to action

As the debate goes on over who is to blame for the problem of media vio-lence and whose responsibility it is to deal with it, children are growing up with the harmful effects. When parents' efforts are constantly being undermined, it is time to stop telling mothers and fathers that they are not doing their job. Curbing the effects of media is a job parents cannot possibly do on their own. It is time to put aside the debate about whose fault media violence is and for all those who care about children to take action to combat the hazards of media culture.

CHAPTER 2

How Children Experience
Media Violence and Media Culture:
A Developmental Perspective

A mother recounted the following incident, which took place during the United States invasion of Haiti:

> A radio report about the attack came on during our family breakfast. Suddenly, 6-year-old Brian jumped up and said, "I sure hope we have the Power Rangers there to help." I reminded Brian that the Power Rangers were only pretend. He responded, "I know. But they can take off their [Power Ranger] outfits and then go fight." Immediately, 4-year-old Rosemarie chimed in, "Yeah, and they better have the Megazoids [the Power Rangers' most powerful weapon] with them too."
>
> Both children began prancing around the kitchen pretending to karate-chop each other like the Power Rangers do. Just as my husband and I asked them to stop, one of Brian's karate chops caught Rosemarie's arm, and she burst into tears.

How children learn

Children build ideas about the world through a slow process of construction. They do not passively absorb information and ideas. They take content that they see and hear and transform it into something meaningful to them. And the meaning they make builds onto what they have already figured out from prior experience.

The manner in which Brian and Rosemarie deal with what they hear about the invasion of Haiti graphically illustrates this process. They hear something on the news about the fighting in Haiti and try to figure it out. They do this by connecting what they just heard to something they already learned about fighting, in this case from the TV show *The Mighty Morphin Power Rangers*. For instance, Rosemarie knows the pretend Megazoid is the Power Rangers' most powerful weapon, so in any fighting that must be what is needed. Brian knows the Power Rangers are strong and always win, so he decides they are needed to fight with the good guys (the U.S. troops).

Wherever children get the content, whether or not it is violent, they need to go through this kind of process to make their experience meaningful. And often, as children go through that process, we can learn a lot of useful information about what they are thinking and learning.

How young children think

As Rosemarie and Brian try to make sense of what they hear about the fighting in Haiti, they reveal several of the special characteristics of young children's thinking that affect how they interpret their experience.

They do not fully distinguish pretend and real. They use what they have learned from a fictional show about good guys and bad guys and about fighting and weapons to interpret something they hear about real-world violence. The fact that Brian has often been told that the Power Rangers are mere actors does not stop him from giving them "real" soldier status.

They focus on the dramatic, concrete aspects of the situation—not the more abstract concepts underlying the war. The fighting and weapons are what they gravitate to, not the underlying issues.

They do not make logical causal connections. As they focus on the action and excitement of the fighting, Rosemarie and Brian do not think about the pain and suffering that might result.

They focus on only one aspect of the situation at a time. Their thinking is more like a series of separate slides rather than like a movie. They do not think about the whole picture—the context for the fighting—why there is fighting or what may be the possible outcomes.

They think in terms of dichotomous, all-or-nothing categories. In fights someone either "wins" or "loses." There are good guys and bad guys; the Power Rangers are clearly "good," while whomever they are fighting is "bad." Furthermore, anything the "good" side does seems to be unquestionably "right" and anything the "bad" side does is "wrong."

To illustrate many of the characteristics of young children's thinking described above, here is an example of 5-year-old Henry's thinking about the movie *Star Wars*. The accompanying commentary points out these characteristics as well as the techniques the teacher (T) uses to explore Henry's (H) thinking.

Dialogue	Commentary
T: Tell me about what you're making with the Legos.	Throughout, the teacher uses open-ended questions to explore Henry's thinking.
H: Star Wars spaceships with lasers.	He focuses on the most salient and powerful feature of the spaceship—the laser.
T: Who uses the spaceships?	
H: Han Solo and Chewbacca.	
T: What do they use the spaceships for?	
H: To fly in space. They go on their own. [Each has a spaceship.]	Henry has chosen one salient aspect of the movie to focus on—a spaceship for each character.
T: What do they do in their spaceships?	The teacher's questions stay focused on concrete actions, not abstract ideas.
H: Shoot bad guys if the bad guys are coming right toward them.	He uses dichotomous categories for good and bad guys.
T: What do they shoot?	She explores his thinking without making a value judgment on the fighting.
H: Bullets.	He focuses on one thing—shooting, not the illogic of lasers shooting bullets.
T: And then what happens?	
H: Then if a bullet hits them they blow up. These go back [pointing to movable Lego flaps].	He focuses on the most salient, dramatic aspect of the shooting—the "blowing up," not the loss of life.
T: What did the bad guys do to make the good guys shoot the bullets at them?	She tries to get him to focus on the causality—what bad thing prompted the shooting.
H: They have things that can shoot out, and this is where they shoot out.	He stays focused on the concrete characteristics, not the underlying causes.
T: Why do the good guys need to shoot?	She again tries to get him to focus on the underlying causes.

(continued on next page)

(continued from p. 25)

Dialogue	Commentary
H: To blow up the bad guys because they are mean to the good guys and the bad guys want to kill the good guys.	He uses dichotomous and static thinking—bad guys do bad things because they are "mean" and "kill."
T: Do you know why they want to kill the good guys?	She tries to get at underlying causality.
H: Because they're not on the good guys' team.	He is still focusing on one thing at a time—good and bad—by adding teams to the dichotomous categories; "killing" is not connected to real-world meanings or effects.
T: Oh, so there's two teams, a good guys' team and a bad guys' team?	She reflects his thinking back to him to see if he goes further with it.
H: Yeah, and Darth Vader is on the dark side and Luke Skywalker is on the light side.	He continues to focus exclusively on good and bad and uses concrete, tangible information to further define his dichotomous categories.
T: Is that how you can tell who is on what team, by the colors that they wear?	She seeks clarification of his thinking.
H: Well, well, not, well . . . I know because my friend Paul told me. He has lot of Star Wars toys, and he told me about the dark side. Some of Darth Vader's slaves have white on, but they're bad guys.	The teacher's question has Henry a bit confused and gets him outside of the focus on fighting. He is trying to make sense out of his friend's information, but still focuses on the concrete. There's also confusion about how both bad and good guys can wear white.

Learning lessons about violence from the media

Children learn about how to treat each other and how to deal with their problems and conflicts with others through the same process of construction described above. They try out the behaviors and ideas to which they are exposed to see how they work. Then they modify them based on the results of what they try. Children gradually build up a repertoire of ideas and behaviors about how people treat each other. I have found it helpful to think of this repertoire as being like a file box. Children use their experience to create a catalog of information about behavior. When they have a new experience, they pull out the file card that, in their mind, best matches the situation.

The content of the file cards children develop is highly influenced by how they see the people around them—both through direct experience and through the media—dealing with each other and their conflicts. Brian and Rosemarie's behavior illustrates this repertoire-building process. As they hear about the Haiti invasion, they use an idea about fighting and violence they have gotten from the Mighty Morphin Power Rangers—on the TV program, in the movie, and maybe even in video games; the "pretend" violence the Power Rangers commit is okay to use use in real-world conflicts. Similarly, as Brian and Rosemarie exchange karate chops, pretending to be Power Rangers fighting in Haiti, they are using a behavior from their repertoire that they associate with fighting. When Rosemarie gets hurt, perhaps they also will learn something about the potentially harmful effects of violent behavior.

Right now, children are being bombarded with violent content in the media—both entertainment and news—that they use to build their repertoire. This content shows them that violent responses to conflict are powerful, exciting, and preferred methods of solving problems with other people. It also promotes a repertoire that often makes our advice to "use words, not fists" to solve problems seem weak and ineffectual.

The characteristics of thinking described above make young children particularly susceptible to the lessons about violence they see on the screen. For instance, research suggests that when a media character engages in violence that does not have a negative consequence for that character or the victim, it most likely will promote learning of violent attitudes and behaviors.[24] Because young children tend to focus on one aspect of a situation at a time and do not connect the scenes of a story into a logical sequence, they often ignore the context in which violence occurs and what happens to a character who commits or is a victim of violence.

A Developmental Framework for Assessing Children's Television

Developmental Issues	What Children See on TV	What Children Should See
Establish a sense of trust and safety	A dangerous world, with enemies everywhere. Weapons needed to feel safe.	A world in which people can be trusted and help each other, where safety and predictability can be achieved, where fears can be overcome.
Develop a sense of autonomy with connectedness	Autonomy equated with fighting and weapons. Connectedness equated with helplessness, weakness, and altruism.	A wide range of models of independence within meaningful relationships and of autonomous people helping each other.
Develop a sense of empowerment and efficacy	Physical strength and violence equals power and efficacy. Bad guys always return. Alternative ways to have an impact are *not* shown.	Many examples of people having a positive effect on their world without using violence.
Establish gender identity	Exaggerated, rigid gender divisons—boys are strong, violent, saviors of the world; girls are helpless, victimized, and irrelevant to world events.	Compex characters with wide-ranging behaviors, interests, and skills; commonalities between the sexes overlapping in what both can do.
Develop an appreciation of diversity among people	Racial and ethnic stereotyping and dehumanized enemies. Diversity is dangerous. Violence against those who are different is justified.	Diverse peoples with varied talents, skills, and needs, who treat each other with respect, work out problems nonviolently, and enrich each others' lives.
Construct the foundations of morality and social responsibility	One-dimensional characters who are all good or bad. Violence is the solution to interpersonal problems. Winning is the only acceptable outcome. Bad guys deserve to be hurt.	Complex characters who act responsibly and morally toward others—showing kindness and respect, working out moral problems, considering other people's points of view.
Have opportunities for meaningful play	Program content far removed from children's experience or level of understanding. Program-linked toys promoting imitative, not creative, play.	Meaningful content to use in play that resonates deeply with developmental needs; shows not linked to realistic toys so that children can create their own unique play.

Source: Adapted from D. Levin and N. Carlsson-Paige, "Developmentally Appropriate Television: Putting Children First," *Young Children* 49 (July 1994): 38–44.

Furthermore, because young children are often drawn to the most graphic and dramatic aspects of a situation, the more extreme a program, the more it grabs children's attention. Children, an especially receptive and attentive audience, are captivated by the quick-paced and visually graphic action so common in violence that occurs on the screen.

The chart on page 28 provides an example of the lessons children can learn from violent media in one key area: conflict resolution. By way of contrast, the chart also describes what children need to learn to solve problems peacefully.

ACTION IDEA

Use the chart on page 28 to guide decisions about appropriate and inappropriate media for children. It can also help you see the kinds of information you can incorporate into your work with children to help counteract the negative messages of media violence.

Challenges to finding an effective response

After the Haitian invasion, Brian and Rosemarie's parents made conscientious efforts to limit the amount of television their children watch and to limit their exposure to media violence. While an essential part of any approach, *trying to protect children from exposure is rarely enough*; some messages simply permeate children's environment—not just on the screen but in daily life. Children need to make sense of those media messages about fighting and violence that do get through, and as they do, they run the risk of learning negative lessons. Teachers and parents have an essential role to play in minimizing that risk.

At the same time, you probably will not be surprised to hear that when it comes to media-related issues, getting children to think and behave as we would like is not a simple matter. As we have seen, children do not think the way adults do, nor do they simply take in adult ideas and information and "learn" them. Rather, they actively make their own unique meanings and transform what we try to teach them in their own unique ways. We need to recognize this fundamental way of thinking and learning and take it into account in any interaction we have with media violence or other issues.

We also need to recognize that because of how children think, they often are most attracted to those aspects of media and toys that we most want to protect them from—the most fast paced, graphic in detail, and violent. We have to accept children's fascination with the violent popular culture as we try to find ways to help them cope.

Practical guidelines to keep in mind

As we work with children to reduce the role of media and media violence in their lives and to counteract the negative lessons they are learning from it, keep in mind the following guidelines to increase the effectiveness of our efforts. Each strategy offered in this book to help counteract the harmful lessons of media and media violence is built upon the ideas about young children's thinking and learning described in this chapter.

Guidelines for Working with Children on Media Issues

• This is a slow, complex, and ongoing process. *Ideas and decisions you make with your children will need to be revised* as children grow and develop and circumstances change.

   In the description of Brian's reaction to the invasion of Haiti at the beginning of the chapter, Brian was told that the Power Rangers are not real. He still decides they should go to fight. When his mother pushes him to deal with the fact that they are only pretend, he takes his thinking a step further by dealing with what he thinks makes them pretend—their costumes. But Brian still has a long way to go before he can sort out the fantasy and reality of TV characters as adults can.

• Because young children learn by doing, the more you can *embed what you do into children's everyday lives* and experiences, the more powerful your lessons will be.

   The teacher who talks to Henry about the *Star Wars* movie connects it to what he is actually doing with the Legos. This helps give a meaningful focus to the discussion. A next step for the teacher might be to help Henry compare and contrast what he says the Star Wars characters do with what he does in his own life.

• The more you can *find out about what children think and the unique meanings they have made,* the more you can help them find meaningful ways to connect what you want them to learn to what they already know. This helps bring about real change in thinking and behavior. And it can help you respect and take into account the cultural diversity and individual experiences of the children.

   The teacher's discussion with Henry about Star Wars shows how to go about collecting the kind of information you need to work with children in unique and respectful ways.

• Few efforts will *ever* go as planned nor will they go the same way twice. *What is important is that children be encouraged to say what they think,* that you try to use and build on their ideas and come up with solutions and conclusions together.

   Henry's teacher does not know where her questions about Star Wars will lead, and she takes her cues from his responses. She does this without making the kinds of value judgments about fighting that might make him feel it is not okay to say what he really thinks.

• Rather than trying to get children to think as adults do about media issues and just giving them adult ideas about media in simpler words, help them work out their own ideas. *Broaden the range and complexity of ideas* and information children have to draw on as they formulate their own views. In particular, include input that challenges harmful lessons conveyed through the media.

   Here again, in the example about the invasion of Haiti, the mother stimulated Brian to think in somewhat more complex terms when she pointed out that the Power Rangers were not real. So did Henry's teacher when, at the end of the Star Wars discussion, he began to deal with the complexity of the color white not just being for the good guys. Many other examples of teachers working to further children's thinking are sprinkled throughout this book.

CHAPTER 3

Getting Ready to Take Action

Finding effective ways to make a lasting impact on how media, media violence, and media culture affect children is a very challenging endeavor. Usually, such strategies are not obvious by intuition. And there are no simple solutions that will make the problems of media and media violence go away. Promoting healthy development, learning, and behavior in the midst of the violent media and popular culture is an ongoing process. It presents endless variations that cannot all be fully predicted or planned for.

A flexible, multifaceted approach generally serves everyone's interests best. Here are a few background steps that can provide a grounding for your efforts with children.

WHAT YOU CAN DO

Learn about the TV programs and other media in children's lives.

When you are familiar with the TV shows, videos, movies, and computer games that the children in your setting are experiencing, you are better able to notice when and how these enter children's thoughts and actions and how to discuss them intelligently with children.

ACTION IDEA

Make a videotape of a couple of episodes of each of the most popular TV programs your children watch.

- Watch them at a convenient time and in doses that you can handle. Become familiar with the main characters, props, and plots. Try to figure out the messages and meanings children are likely to get. Also watch the commercials to get a sense of the toys and other products being promoted to children.

- Watch the tapes with other teachers and/or parents so you can discuss and analyze them as well as develop strategies for working with and talking to children about them.

Learn about media-linked toys and other related products
(such as lunch boxes or shoes) your children own or desire.

Children learn from their play; what and how they play influences how they learn. Toys are powerful tools in influencing what and how children play. Since many of the most popular toys sold today are linked to the media, we would expect them to have a big influence on what and how many children play. Moreover, it's reasonable to assume that media-linked toys multiply the impact of viewing since they enable children to play out, over and over again, what they saw—including the violence.

Because of the power that toys can exert over children's play, knowing the toys children are playing with can help you understand more fully how media violence is entering their lives and what messages they may be learning. This knowledge will also help you devise strategies for responding. (The issue of toys and play is discussed more fully in Chapter 6.)

The following list from a toy trade magazine shows where toy dollars are going. As you can see, most of them are linked to one or more type of media.

Best-Selling Toy Lines (October 1996)

1. Barbie[M, T] (e.g., Baywatch Barbie, based on the *Baywatch* TV show)

2. Lego Basic

3. Star Wars[M, V]

4. Mighty Morphin Power Rangers[M, T, V]

5. Sesame Street[T]

6. Hot Wheels

7. Toy Story[M]

8. Batman[M, T, V]

9. Mortal Kombat[M, V]

10. Nerf (including the "Chainblazer Blaster" and an entire line of toy weapons)

M = Toys with a link to movies
T = Toys with a link to television
V = Toys with a link to video and computer games

Source: *Playthings: The International Merchandising Magazine of the Toy Industry,* January 1997.

Visit a mass-market toy store to survey toys currently being marketed to children.

- Notice what toys are featured in special displays.

- Read the backs of toy boxes.

- Try to find the messages that tell what toys are for boys and girls and how children should play.

- Observe interactions among children and adults to see what toys children choose and how they choose.

You also can visit a video store and video-game arcade to learn more about other media entering children's lives.

This illustration of an action figure/ monster in the Godzilla toy line comes from a toy store's Website. The description is similar to those found on the boxes of many media-linked action figures. Such toy descriptions are readily available on the Internet.

Caught in the powerflux of Dr. Shiragami's Re-Genesis trap, Godzilla lay at the bottom of the sea. Nuclear missiles from mankind's mightiest submarines struck multiple hits on the great Monster while Tazer Subs pumped billions of volts of electricity into his unconscious form. But Godzilla's nuclear-based body absorbed the vast energies of destruction! Godzilla rose more mighty than ever; the blackened color of his skin a testament to the super powers within!

Here is the back of the box for a toy linked to the movie **Independence Day.** *Recommended for children age 4 and up, the toy comes equipped with a replica of such New York City buildings as the Empire State Building, the Statue of Liberty, and the World Trade Center. It also comes with a computer disk so children can blow up the city on screen.*

Use the following Media Profile for Parents to learn about the role media and media violence is playing in the lives of your children.

This media survey can provide a baseline of information for setting goals and devising strategies for promoting reflection, discussion, and change. If you are a teacher, it can help you tailor your approach to the special characteristics, experiences, and attitudes of the children and families in your program. In many cases the very process of completing the questionnaire will start this reflection and discussion process among family members.

Media Profile for Parents

1. How many television sets does your family own? Where in the house are they located?

2. How many hours a day do your children watch TV? What kinds of TV shows do they watch? What shows are their favorites?

3. Does your family own a VCR or an electronic game system? How much time does your child/ren spend using them? What are their favorite videos and video games?

4. Does your family have access to the Internet/World Wide Web? How, when, and for what purposes is it used in your family?

5. When do your children watch TV or use other media?

6. Do you ever watch TV, play video games, or use the computer with your children? If so, when?

7. Do you have any TV, video games, or computer guidelines or rules? If so, what are they and how well do you think they are working?

8. What do your children like to do when they are not watching TV or doing other media activities?

9. When not watching TV, what kinds of activities does your family like to do together?

10. What are your children's favorite toys? Are any of them linked to TV shows or movies? Have you noticed any differences in how your children play with different kinds of toys?

11. How do you feel about the role that TV and video games play in your children's lives? Is there anything you would like to change? If so, please describe.

12. How many children do you have and what are their ages? Does this create any issues for your family around TV watching?

13. Is there anything else you would like to say about media in your child's and family's life?

Think about how to get other parents, teachers, and community members involved in your efforts to deal with media and media violence that affect children.

It can be very difficult to work on this issue alone. Sharing ideas, successes, and failures with others provides energy to keep you going and helps develop effective strategies tailored to your own unique circumstances. When adults join together, it also is much easier to influence children's developing ideas and behaviors.

In my own efforts to get others involved, I have found almost nothing but appreciation and relief when adults find structured and manageable ways to work with children on media and media violence issues. The chapters at the end of this book are full of concrete activities on which we all can work together.

Action Idea

Modify and use the sample letters in Chapters 9 and 11 to educate and enlist other adults to your cause. Organize an informal meeting to discuss with other parents and/or teachers the ideas in this book that seem the most relevant to your situation.

Examine the role media plays in your own life.

Use the questions on the following page to explore your own experiences with media.

Questions to Help Adults Explore the Role of Media in Their Own Lives

- How do media contribute to and detract from my own life outside of work?

- Are there things about the media in my life would I like to change? How can I begin to make the changes?

- How well do I understand the media: how it is made, why it is made the way it is, how it affects my ideas about the world? Are there other adults with whom I can discuss these issues? What media-related issues would I like to know more about?

- How can my own experiences with media and feelings about its role in my life help me better understand what the experiences of media are like for children?

PART II

WORKING WITH CHILDREN IN CLASSROOM SETTINGS

4

Helping Children Make Sense of Media and Media Violence

While the amount and influence varies, media and technology are a part of the lives of children growing up today and are likely to become even more so. Some media, when used appropriately, promise to provide children with positive opportunities for growth and learning, but much is worrisome.

Even our best efforts to use media in children's best interests and to protect them from inappropriate material will not fully shield them from violence and other potentially harmful aspects of media. And even if we could successfully shield them when they are young from the problems created by media, children need our help learning how to process and use the media they do see. And as children grow older and take more control of their lives, they will need resources and skills to become responsible and literate consumers of media. We need to develop strategies that effectively help children cope now and in the future.

Engaging children in meaningful dialogues about media and media violence

As the following example illustrates, the task for teachers and parents is not one of imparting information or a set of right answers. The challenge is to help children explore the possible answers in ways they can understand and see how to connect them to their own ideas and behaviors.

As discussed in earlier chapters, children need many opportunities to try out the new ideas, to see how they work, to make their own connections to what they already know, and to come to their own conclusions according to their past experiences and level of development.

Creating an ongoing process

The kind of process to aim for is poignantly illustrated by this teacher's account of a lesson that was part of a thematic curriculum project on TV advertising.

> We did an experiment identifying differing brands of cola sodas—those that were and were not advertised on TV. Children were blindfolded and asked to taste and identify four different brands (Pepsi, Coke, and two generic colas). They were surprised and even frustrated to find that they could not identify the brands accurately. They wanted to repeat the taste test several times to make sure they would get the same results. Reluctantly, they agreed they could not tell the difference among the brands.
>
> Then at lunch time, when I gave the children the remaining cola to drink, a near brawl ensued over who would get the Coke and Pepsi. No one wanted to drink the generic brands. I was really discouraged. Hadn't they learned anything from the earlier science taste-test experiment?
>
> Suddenly Camilla grinned and said, "I know, let's all eat lunch with blindfolds, and then we won't fight!"

This teacher, having taught his lesson, assumed that the children learned that all colas tasted about the same despite the advertising they saw on TV. But soon afterward, he was forced to question his conclusion; he was reminded that, because of how young children think and learn, one experience was not enough to get the children to grasp and generalize what they had learned. This does not mean that the lesson was a failure. Camilla shows why. She brings in something from her direct experience with the experiment—use of the blindfold to make all colas the same—to help solve the conflict of sharing cola at lunch. She finds a way to meaningfully connect prior learning with a new challenge. As she does, she helps all the children use what they learned earlier. Camilla and the other children are building ideas about how advertising affects their behavior, a process that will gradually approximate adult thinking.

This kind of give-and-take idea building illustrates the kind of learning to aim for as we teach children to be responsible consumers of media.

WHAT YOU CAN DO

An essential part of helping children become *responsible* consumers of media—individuals who are able to resist the potentially negative ways media can have an impact on their attitudes, values, and behavior—is helping them become *informed* consumers—people who understand the nature and potential effects of media. Learning to look carefully at media and at media's role in their lives can help children become informed consumers. But because of how young children think and learn, this takes a long time and can be a real challenge.

The guidelines and action ideas described below will help you begin. The information and skills children learn will serve as the foundation they need to begin to take the kinds of actions described in the following chapter for dealing effectively with the media in their lives.

Talk to children about TV and find out their likes, dislikes, and viewing habits.

As with the Media Profile for Parents, collecting information from children about the media in their lives can provide you with valuable information about the children's experience, thinking, and needs. It also can help guide your decisions about what to do. You can have a discussion or series of discussions with children, using open-ended questions like those listed on page 46. They will help you learn a lot from the children and also provide a way to get the children thinking about media issues in a safe, nonthreatening way.

Group discussions provide opportunities for children to hear and discuss each other's responses and learn that there is a wide range of possible answers. This exposure to diverse ideas can help them consider new possibilities for themselves. Use the following questions to help guide your discussions with children about the media.

Children's Discussion Questions

1. What TV shows do you like to watch a lot? What do you like about them?

2. What TV shows do you not like to watch? What don't you like about them?

3. When do you watch TV?

4. How do you decide what to watch?

5. What other kinds of screen-time activities do you do besides watching TV programs: videos? video games? computer games? movies?

6. Do you or your parents have any guidelines or rules about your TV watching—such as about what you can watch or when? If so, tell us about them. What do you think about them?

7. What do you like to do when you're not watching TV?

Here is an example of how one child completed a TV Questionnaire that was distributed in her third-grade class at the start of a curriculum unit on media.

TV Questionnaire

Name three of your favorite TV shows.
Rode Roles
Sabrina the teenage witch
All that

What do you like about these shows?
Because there funny
and exsiting.

What TV shows do you dislike?
Beaves and Butthead
Power Rangers
Oprah

Why do you dislike these shows?
Because there borring.

When do you watch TV?
After 6:00

Who do you watch TV with?
My brothers

Where do you watch TV?
the
In   livingroon

What other screen time activities do you enjoy (videos, video games, computer games, movies)?
Computer
Nintendo 64
Game Boy
Moives

Do you have any rules about TV at your house (certain shows you're not allowed to watch or amount of time you're allowed to watch TV)? Any rules or guidelines you can think of?
I not alowed to watch B&B and the Simpsons!
I not alowed to watch TV tell after 6:00.

What do you think about these rules?
I don't like that I can't watch tell 6:00 because when it's 6:00 we are eating after that I have to do dishes after dishes I go to bed so I don't get to watch TV in the week.

What do you like to do when you're not watching TV?
Knit
Computer
Read
Play Piano
Play Flute
Cook

For children who read and write, use some of these discussion questions to make a Child Media Survey Questionnaire that children complete before or after the discussion. Send the questionnaire home and ask children and parents to complete it together.

Do surveys of classmates' responses to the various questions. Children might even graph the results and discuss them at a meeting. They can look for patterns and diversity in responses. Individual children or groups of children can each have a question to survey and graph.

When surveys are done in school, help parents become involved in the discussion by having children share their survey responses at home.

Talk openly with children about media violence and listen carefully to what they have to say.

One of the following letters can help structure beginning discussions with children about media violence. The first letter is for younger children. The second is appropriate for older children.

A Letter from Teachers to Children about Violence on TV and in Movies

Dear Kids:

A lot of children really love to watch TV and videos. Many of the shows they watch have lots of fighting. The fighting seems fun and exciting and like a great way to solve problems.

Many teachers are worried about the violence children see on TV. They say a lot of kids act out the fighting they see on TV when they play. Teachers also say they think TV fighting is making more kids use fighting to solve their conflicts with each other.

Kids often answer, "But we're only pretending. It isn't real. We're just playing." They say pretend violence is different from real fighting.

But teachers say that when children pretend to fight like TV characters, some kids really get hurt. And sometimes kids seem surprised when this happens.

Some kids agree they're surprised when someone gets hurt. They say they're the good guys, and good guys have to fight bad guys—that's why they fight.

A lot of little kids look up to good-guy TV characters and want to do what they do. So the teachers think violent TV shows can teach kids that it's okay to fight and hurt people.

Because teachers are worried about TV violence and kids are getting hurt, we want to help grown-ups and children talk together about it and decide what to do so everyone stays safe.

- What do you think about what teachers are saying?
- What do you think grown-ups should do about violence on TV and in videos?
- What can grown-ups do to help children be safe and learn not to fight?
- What can you do?

Thanks for talking about our letter.

From Many Teachers All Over the Country

A Letter from Children to Children about Violence in the Media

Dear Kids:

We're sixth and seventh graders in Youth Enlightening Youth. We teach younger children about what worries us about violence on TV.

Before we joined Youth Enlightening Youth, grown-ups told us that TV violence was bad for us. They said that TV violence makes it look like violence is fun and exciting and teaches us to use fighting to solve our problems. We got tired of hearing grown-ups complain. So we decided to find out more about media violence ourselves.

We began by keeping track of how much violence we saw. We were really surprised by how much violence there is on TV, in movies, videos, and video games. On most shows the good guys keep fighting the bad guys over and over again. Nothing ever gets settled, and no one ever gets hurt or punished for killing people. This isn't anything like the real world where people need to work out their problems with each other so that no one gets hurt or killed.

We learned that violent TV does teach us that violence is the best way to solve problems. And we don't like that lesson at all. Most of the time, when we have conflicts with our friends, we don't want to hurt them because we care about them.

So we have been working to change things. Now when we watch TV, we try to find really good shows that are not violent. We use a TV schedule to help us choose. We find good videos in our local library. We also find other things to do besides watching TV.

We have started writing letters to the people who make TV shows to tell them what we think. We also try to teach others about what we've learned. That's why we're writing this letter to you.

• What do you think about what we say here in our letter?

• What do you do, besides fighting, to solve conflicts with friends?

• What can you do instead of watching violence on TV, videos, and video games?

• What do you think grown-ups and kids should do about media violence?

Thanks for reading our letter.

From Members of Youth Enlightening Youth

As a follow-up activity, ask children to draw or paint a picture about some aspect of the discussion. It might be about a TV show or character they think is violent or one they think demonstrates alternatives to being violent. Or it can depict a toy that goes with a violent TV show. It could be a poster with a message about what they think. Older children can write about their drawings. Adults can write down younger children's ideas.

Children draw their reactions to the letters about media violence. Their pictures represent pro and con positions on media violence and toys. The teacher accepted both children's views. Creating an environment in which children can honestly express what they think and feel, rather than voice a particular position, is a crucial part of work with children on media issues.

Videotape a few segments of popular children's TV programs. Together, watch and talk about them to help children connect the themes raised in earlier discussions to the programs they actually watch. This also will help children develop a framework and language for talking about media with others. The questions for parents in Chapter 10 on talking about media content with children can help guide your discussion.

Help children learn to participate in regular give-and-take group discussions about media, media violence, and other meaningful topics at a level appropriate to their development.

Leading give-and-take discussions with children about media and media violence issues in which there is no one right answer can be a real challenge. It takes practice and a willingness to take risks—you will not always know where a discussion will lead.

Here is a sample give-and-take discussion about Power Ranger play. This teacher-led discussion about violence in *The Mighty Morphin Power Rangers,* a popular children's TV program, illustrates the kinds of things to aim for in a discussion on media and media violence with young children. It also illustrates how to build onto discussions about violence in the media after you have read and discussed one of the previous letters. The discussion is especially effective because it arises directly out of children's daily classroom experiences.

Problem-Solving Discussion: Taming the Power Rangers[25]

Teacher: I've noticed a problem and I need your help figuring out how to solve it. You know how a lot of children have been playing Power Rangers outside lately? [Several children nod agreement.] Well, when you play Power Rangers, almost all you do is run around and fight. I don't like it when you spend so much time fighting. I want to know what you think about that.

Jenna: I hate them. I never play.

Teacher: Yes, some of you don't like Power Rangers and never play and some of you play a lot. Let's talk about what happens when you do play.

Henry: They fight. The Power Rangers need to fight—that's what they do.

Teacher: Can you tell us about why they need to fight?

Henry: To kill the monsters.

Lai Ling: I hate when they [the Power Rangers] fight. They're so mean.

Teacher: Can you tell us more about how they are mean?

Lai Ling: They yell in your face and they kick and punch. I hate them!

Teacher: So you *really* don't like their noise and their kicking.

Karlís: But that's what Power Rangers do. They *neeeed* to fight.

Teacher: So it sounds like there is a problem. The children playing Power Rangers like to play fight, but other children don't like it when the Power Rangers come near them. It's hard to feel safe when all that fighting and noise is near you and you're trying to do something else.

We need to find something to do about the Power Rangers so no one gets hurt—so that *everyone* feels safe. Does anyone have any ideas about how we could do that? You've come up with really good ideas before about how to solve problems like this.

Sammy: Play somewhere else.

Teacher: You mean Power Rangers should play away from other children? [Sammy nods.]

Riannan: Use your words.

Teacher: So what are some of the words you could use?

Mark: Say, "Go away."

Gilda: Say, "Don't hit" or "Be quiet."

Henry: Say, "No play fighting at school"—like at my day care.

Karlís: Oh brother. [There are a few other groans.]

Teacher: Karlís, it sounds like you don't like that idea. Tell us more.

Karlís: They need to fight. That's what they do.

Teacher: I know the Power Rangers fight a lot. The Power Rangers spend an awful lot of time fighting. That worries me. I wonder what other things they do besides fight.

Hung Mi: They go to high school.

Jenna: They eat in a big room.

Darcy: Hey, the Power Rangers could eat at our restaurant [set up in the dramatic play area].

Teacher: You've really worked hard on this problem and come up with a lot of good ideas. What if we try some of them tomorrow to see how they work? For you who want to play Power Rangers, what if we choose a special place outside where you can play away from the others? Do you think you could try that? [Several nod.] And inside, do children want to use the restaurant to make a meal for the Power Rangers? They must get really hungry. [More nod].

Hung Mi: But it better be something we like to eat!

Teacher: [Nodding and smiling] You've been sitting for a long time. Let's try these two new ideas. I like it that the inside Power Rangers will have something to do besides fighting. We'll talk about how things go at our end-of-day meeting tomorrow.

In addition to illustrating an effective way to lead problem-solving discussions on media issues with young children, this example also illustrates key components of a peaceful conflict-resolution process. Children can learn to use peaceful conflict resolution to counteract the violent-conflict lessons they often learn from the media.[26] Here is a summary of these elements.

Key Elements of Peaceful Conflict Resolution

- *Seeing a problem* as shared by both sides.

- *Coming up with possible solutions* and using words to explore them.

- *Finding a solution* that everyone can agree to try because everybody wins—gets their need met.

- *Trying out* the agreed-upon solution and *seeing how it works* by directly experiencing the consequences.

- *Evaluating* how the solution worked and deciding if and how to change it to make it work better.

- *Using what was learned* to work out future problems and conflicts.

When leading give-and-take discussions with children, keep the following guidelines in mind.

1. Create an atmosphere in which children feel safe in expressing diverse ideas. To enter into a meaningful discussion that can help children learn how to reflect on media and violence issues, children need to feel safe saying what they really think. Otherwise they may just parrot what they think we want to hear or stay out of the discussion rather than begin to honestly reflect on and develop new strategies and approaches for thinking about the issues (the *real* goal for such discussions).

2. Help children put their ideas into words and share them with others through give-and-take dialogue. Expressing one's ideas in a way others can understand is a real challenge for young children. When a child says, "The Power Rangers hurt me," you might say, "You mean, when you were outside and some children were playing Power Rangers, they hurt you with a karate chop?" Or, if a child says, "I don't hurt," you might

say, "Do you mean, when you play Power Ranger games, you don't karate-chop anyone?" This helps all the children understand what is being said and allows them to follow the discussion.

3. Ask open-ended questions that have many possible answers and respect the diverse ways in which children respond. A goal of this kind of discussion is to help children gradually learn to be critical TV viewers and to use media responsibly. Answering questions that don't have one right answer—and hearing others' answers to the questions—is one way that children build up a data base of understanding. The questions listed at the end of the previous letters provide open-ended questions that will help you get started. Try to come up with follow-up questions of your own to help children take their ideas further.

4. Ask questions and bring in information or ideas that provoke children to think in more complex terms. One effective way to help children learn new ideas is to bring in ideas that *challenge* (but do not put down or correct) their thinking. The teachers in the first letter emphasized this approach; when the children talked about their fighting play being "only pretend," the teachers pointed out that even when fighting is pretend, some children *really* get hurt.

5. When possible, end discussions with a concrete plan of action. Coming up with some ideas about what to do after the discussion helps children learn how to explore issues further, solve problems, and change their behavior—crucial steps in learning to resist the negative effects of media and media violence. After reading and discussing the second letter, older children might agree to keep track of the violence they see on TV and come back and report the results at a follow-up discussion the next day. Opportunities for further action also help children learn that they have the *power* to change things. (See Chapter 8.)

ACTION IDEA

Tape your discussions with children about media and media violence. Listen to the recordings to reflect on how the dialogue went and to build onto it later. The recording also will help you reflect on what the children said so you can develop ideas about what to do next.

Here is an example of a teacher's discussion with children about the media that is in keeping with the guidelines outlined above.

During a discussion with 5- to 7-year-olds about TV programs and movies they could and could not watch in their homes, one child mentioned a show that she wished she had not seen. The children ended up discussing "Have you *ever* watched anything you wish you hadn't?" Here is a summary of their responses. Most of the episodes they describe occurred when they were younger.

- My brother gets really scared by movies and then he says he isn't. My parents are really careful about what we can watch.

- When I was little, I saw it on TV about a clown who eats people. I wanted to watch because it was about a clown. I got really scared. I still have the pictures in my head. I didn't tell anyone because I snuck [she wasn't supposed to watch the movie].

- Dad rented *Ghostbusters*. I had nightmares for a whole year. I was worried the ghosts would burst through the walls and kill me. Mom got mad.

- I saw *Robocop* and close-ups of *Jaws*. One guy got shot 30 times. I kept thinking about it when I was going to sleep.

- I saw *Cape Fear*. It has a guy who kills a dog. He got drunk. He took this woman home and handcuffed her to the bed and bit her. It wasn't scary—just disgusting. I saw it at my friend's house. Her mom lets her see lots of disgusting stuff.

- We saw *Treasure Island*. I kept going in and out of the room I got so scared.

- When I was younger I saw a show—I can't remember the name—that had a lot of guns and people getting shot. I worried I was going to be murdered like that.

- I was really scared by a skeleton they had on *Sesame Street* that moved.

- I used to watch the news with my dad. It really freaked me out because of all the people who break into your house. I have this back door and worried that people would come in.

- When I was really small, *Bambi* got me really sad when the mother got killed. I remember going to my mom's bed at night.

- I was really embarrassed when I saw *Bambi*. I was really scared and cried, and my friend didn't [both were boys].

This teacher's account illustrates how using the guidelines can lead to rich and meaningful discussions that deeply reflect children's understanding and concerns. The children get to talk about important experiences that they usually have to deal with on their own. And we learn so much about the children. Their responses poignantly reveal that children see a wide range of programming that many adults would consider inappropriate for them. We learn about how what the children see on the screen affects their thoughts, feelings, and behaviors. We also see how children's reactions are not always predictable. For instance, some children are distressed by programming that we generally think of as appropriate for their age group. Finally, these reactions illustrate why it is so important for adults to establish a dialogue with children about the media in their lives: children must have a safe way to talk about these issues and get support to deal with them.

Help children look at what in the media is pretend and what is real.

As we saw when Brian wanted to have the Power Rangers help with the invasion of Haiti (Chapter 2), it is not always easy for children to sort out the fantasy and reality of what they see on the screen. It is especially confusing when shows and movies and, increasingly, video and computer games mix animation and special effects with real-life action and actors (as is the case with shows like *The Mighty Morphin Power Rangers*).

Even though children often tell us what they see in the media is "just pretend," sorting out fantasy from reality is usually a confusing and difficult process that is connected to how they think. Children know best the real things that they have experienced directly. Because they have not experienced many of the things they see in the media, they do not have a lot of information that can help them sort out real from pretend. Similarly, they tend to focus on one thing at a time, and that one thing on the screen is often the most salient thing that is happening at any particular moment. Children usually fail to focus on the whole context in which that event occurred, what happened before or after it, or how it might have been made to happen. This is the kind of information that would help them figure out whether what they are seeing is pretend or real.

Children also need similar information to be able to sort out commercials from actual programs. They also need help figuring out those aspects of a particular program that have to do with the toys and other products that are marketed with the show. Knowing how young children think, media marketing often takes unfair advantage of children's developmental vulnerabilities.[27] In fact, research focusing specifically on advertising has shown that children do not make tidy distinctions between commercials and real life. They also have little understanding of the advertising intent, which makes them especially vulnerable.[28]

While there are limits to what children can understand about fantasy and reality in the media—in both programs and commercials—there are many ways we can help them develop their understanding. Here are a few ideas to help you begin. With younger children, do just one little piece at a time and see where it leads. Older children find it easier to make connections between various aspects of the process.

Ask children open-ended questions about what in the media is pretend and what is real.

Here are examples of the kinds of questions to try:

- Was that pretend or real? How could you tell?

- Has anything like that ever happened to you? Do you think it could?

- How do you think they made that happen? I wonder why the people who made the show/commercial did it that way.

- [If the commercial is for a toy] Do you think the toy would look/work like that if you had it?

Here is an example of how one teacher used a meaningful event that spontaneously came up in her preschool classroom to build an activity about pretend versus real characters. The responses from the 4-year-olds provide a revealing glimpse into just how complicated sorting out what is pretend and what is real in the media can be for young children.

As Halloween approached, the children were talking about what they were going to be on Trick or Treat night. Several mentioned TV and movie characters; others talked about witches, skeletons, and ghosts. When their discussions turned to whether the characters they saw on Halloween really existed, I decided it would be helpful to have a class discussion of these issues.

I designed a bulletin board to assist in our discussion. I divided the board in half with a vertical line. At the bottom of one side I wrote the word *Real* in green and, on the other side, *Pretend* in red. I stuck several push pins into each side. After cutting out and laminating magazine or drawn pictures of many of the characters the children had been discussing, I punched a hole near the top of each character and tied a small yarn loop through it.

I started the discussion by showing the children a picture of a monster. We discussed whether it was real or pretend. The children all agreed it was pretend, so we hung it on a push pin on the pretend side of the board. I started simply with pictures I felt would be agreed upon, then moved to ones that might need some debate. The pictures were of real characters such as farmers, police officers, cooks, and doctors, as well as pretend characters. Here are some examples of the children's ideas.

Witch

"I saw one at a haunted house."

"My mom said it was just someone with a costume on."

[The consensus was that it should be on the pretend side.]

Spider-Man

"He's pretend because he is a cartoon."

Superman

"He is just a man in a costume."

"No, I know he is real because I saw him fly."

"But I saw how he lies down and they move the sky behind him."

[With more discussion the children decided he was pretend and the flying was some sort of trick.]

Ghost

"They are pretend."

"But what about Casper? He isn't scary."

"He's not real. He's a cartoon."

Firefighter

"My daddy's a firefighter."

"Yeah, and he's a real person."

Teacher: "So real people can work as firefighters and still be daddies?"

Ballerina

"They are pretend—they are someone in a costume."

"My sister takes ballet. She has a tutu like that."

Teacher: "So real people can be ballet dancers?"

Skeleton

"It's pretend."

"No, they are real. I have one inside of me."

Teacher: "Can they walk around without skin and muscles?"

"No."

Teacher: "So should we put this skeleton that doesn't have skin and muscles in the pretend area and make a second skeleton that is the inside of a person to hang in the real area?"

Rainbow Bright

"It's pretend 'cause it's a cartoon."

"No, I saw her at the mall."

"That was just a person with a costume on."

"No, she was real because I saw her underwear."

[Since the children couldn't agree, we decided to hang the picture so it overlapped both areas.]

Power Rangers

"Yes, they are real."

"No, they have costumes."

"They can take off their costumes; then they're real."

"I saw the Red Ranger once. It was real."

"But my mom says they're not real."

[The children put this one overlapping both areas too.]

Over the next few weeks the children moved the pictures around as they continued to raise new arguments for why the various characters were pretend or real. And they brought in additional pictures to add to the board.

Help children directly experience various aspects of how TV programs and other media are made.

- Use a tape recorder to experiment with sound effects. Children can record sounds, play them back, decide what they sound like, play guessing games with the sounds, and write their own stories to go with them. They also can make their own sounds to accompany a segment of a TV program, movie, or video.

- Read children *The Bionic Bunny Show* (Brown & Brown 1984), which is about the making of a superhero TV program. The book shows how pretend things are made to look real.

- Flip books can help children understand more about how animation and cartoons work. Simple ones can be purchased, or older children can make their own.

Videotape an episode of a popular children's show. Choose a few segments that use special effects to make fantastic and/or impossible things happen. Help the children try to figure out how the effects were made. (Remember, there are many right answers.)

Take children through a simple media production process.

Help children write their own scripts with words and pictures. Often this works best if you start with interesting experiences the children have had themselves or know a lot about. Encourage children to rewrite familiar scripts to make them less violent, sexist, or racist, or to give them happier endings. Children also enjoy informally acting out their scripts.

If you have a video camera available you can tape the productions. Children can revise and retape their productions and try to bring in special effects and sounds. Taping very simple sequences of action planned by the children also can produce very interesting results.

Use videotaped segments of children's programs (including those from earlier discussions about violence and what is pretend and real) to examine media production techniques more closely.

- Play just the audio part of a small segment of the tape. Ask the children to guess what they think is happening in the picture.

- Show the visual part of the tape without the sound. Ask the children to predict what the sound will be like. Ask them to compose their own sounds.

A special note about connecting media activities to the whole curriculum

One challenge many of us face in implementing these activities in our classrooms is how to add more to the full curriculum we are already supposed to cover. Many of the activities proposed here provide rich and meaningful ways to work on commonly mandated curriculum areas, such as language, reading and writing, math and science. Seeing the connections between media activities and more "standard" curriculum content can enhance how we cover the required curriculum as well as help us justify the media activities to others.

The following curriculum web illustrates the connections between a TV-show production activity and basic curriculum subject areas. Webs like this can be made for other media activities as we integrate the activity into other aspects of children's learning.[29]

Skills Embedded in Making a TV Show with Children

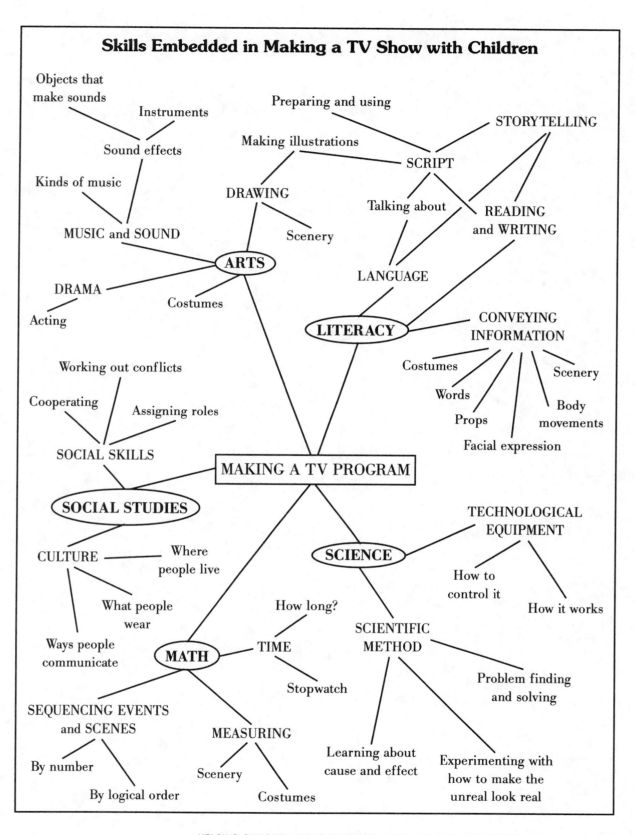

Helping Children Take Charge of the Media in Their Lives

W e can do much to reduce the negative impact of media, media violence, and media culture on children. When we teach children how to take charge of what they watch, give them tools for "reading" the messages beneath the surface and talking about what they see, and help them understand how media work, we can reduce the negative impact of media violence. It is important to help children become knowledgeable and responsible consumers of media and media-related products, to the extent that their level of development allows.

The special challenges of teaching media literacy to young children

Making informed media choices can be quite challenging for young children. Media literacy is developed gradually, only with time, maturity, and experience. The younger children are and the less experience they have had making thoughtful choices, the more help they need from adults.

For instance, to make an informed choice a child needs to know such simple things as what the possible choices are: what shows are on at the time she can watch and what to expect from each show. A child also needs to be able to consider the possible consequences of making a choice: what she won't get to see if she watches a particular program, how she will feel or act during or after it—will it scare her or make her happy?—and what she may miss doing if she watches TV.

Perhaps the biggest challenge to helping children become informed and responsible consumers of media is the nature of media itself. For instance, when children have a few free minutes or are in transition from one activity to the next, they often find it easy to sit down in front of the screen—seeing whatever is on TV or starting up a video game. The screen's fast pace and excitement ensures immediate "entertainment" with little risk or exertion.

Because of how young children think, it is hard for them to resist this powerful lure, and it can quickly become a habit.

Turning off the TV presents similar challenges for many children. It can be very hard for them to make the transition from being passively entertained to actively taking charge of their activity. My family coined the term PTVT (post-TV trauma) to give legitimacy to this experience; then we tried to figure out what to do to help our son deal with it.

Pulling children away from TV programs is a challenge. Children's media are designed to get attention and keep it. The fast, dramatic, and often violent action gets more and more extreme with each new show as producers try to lure children away from rival shows. Turning off video games poses a similar challenge because there is always "just one more thing" to try to achieve in the games.

In addition, marketing practices, with the whole lines of highly realistic toys and other products that accompany children's media, create an environment in which the images from the shows are constantly on many children's minds. The high degree to which these images permeate children's play culture and peer interactions further compounds the difficulty.

WHAT YOU CAN DO

Help children take charge of what they watch.

Teach children how to make good choices about TV programs as well as movies, videos, and video and computer games. Building onto the information obtained in the Children's Discussion Questions (in Chapter 4), you can begin discussions and develop activities that focus on children making conscious choices about their media viewing. Of course, children, as well as adults, have a range of opinions about what is good and bad and what is okay and not okay to watch. When differing ideas are expressed or disagreements occur, rather than looking for the "right" answer, you can help children explore the issues that may underlie the disagreement—in the same way the teacher did in the Power Rangers discussion in the last chapter. The more active the role children play in making decisions about what to watch, the more meaningful and effective those choices are likely to be.

As you work with children, also try to work closely with parents so they can support these efforts in ways that work for their individual families. (See Chapter 9 for suggestions about how to do this.)

Help children learn how to do advance *planning* for their TV watching and other screen time. An essential part of being able to take charge of TV watching and involvement with other media is learning to plan ahead rather than turn on the TV or a video game on impulse.

- *Develop guidelines with children for how much TV they will watch.* Exact amounts of screen time for children vary. Some experts suggest no more than an hour a day for young children.[30] Whatever the amount of time, an overall goal here is to help children keep their TV viewing and other screen time at a level low enough that they do not become dependent on media to fill their free time. In most cases, this means less is better.

  Talk with children about viewing guidelines and limits that their parents have already created, and listen to the children's own ideas about what guidelines should be.

  Because young children's understanding of time is limited, they will need your help here. Often, the number of shows and what times of day to watch are the only kinds of units children can meaningfully discuss.

- *Discuss all types of screen-time activities, including videos, video games, and computer time, if these play a role in the children's lives.* The media in children's lives often go far beyond the viewing of TV programs. In these situations, even when limits on TV viewing are established, other media activities fill much of children's remaining free time. Therefore, when considering how much and what media children will consume, it is important to include all screen-time activities in the discussion and to help figure out how to preserve non-screen-time activities in the midst of all the media options.

- *Help children plan what and when they will watch.* By kindergarten or first grade, children can keep a personal viewing log to plan what they will watch. You can help them make little books in which they can record what they plan to watch and then check off the show.

ACTION IDEA

Children with differing levels of reading/writing ability can keep their TV-viewing books in different ways. For instance, pre- and early readers can draw pictures to represent each show they plan to watch and then circle the art after the show; older children can add such additional details as a schedule of days and times.

Discuss the books on a regular basis: "How did your planning work? Tell me/us about it. What was hard about it? Are there things you would like to change about your planning?" Through such discussion, children can learn about what others have done. They may come up with ideas for changing when and what they watch and for expanding the information they keep in their plan books.

Even before learning to read and write, children can make a Plan for TV Viewing by drawing pictures of the show/s they plan to watch. Adults can help write down program names and times.

PLAN FOR TV VIEWING FOR _____

Day of week	PICTURE OF SHOW #1	PICTURE OF SHOW #2	PICTURE OF SHOW #3
_____	NAME _____ WHEN _____	NAME _____ WHEN _____	NAME _____ WHEN _____
_____	NAME _____ WHEN _____	NAME _____ WHEN _____	NAME _____ WHEN _____

Explore with children how their parents and other adults in their lives deal with TV and other media. Make a list of the rules and guidelines children have for watching TV and using other media at home. Talk with the children about what they think of the rules. Why have parents made them? How are the rules fair? How not? What rules do the children think there should be?

Help the children write a letter home telling their parents what they think are good TV rules. Letting parents know their children's ideas and feelings often paves the way for meaningful discussions and collaborative media rule-making between children and parents.

This chart was generated by kindergartners at the beginning of a discussion of their ideas about TV rules. In a follow-up activity they wrote letters to parents about TV rules.

TV RULES WE HAVE AT HOME

- No TV before school
- No TV after dinner
- No TV during dinner
- Nobody can sit too close to the TV
- No fighting over the best TV chair
- TV on weekends only
- No turning the channel when someone else is watching
- The TV can only be on until 8:30 at night
- You can't turn on the TV just because you're bored
- No blocking anybody else
- Only two shows a day
- No TV that's really scary
- We don't have any rules (three children)

Dear _____,

Today in school we talked about TV rules. I think we should have some TV rules in our house. Here is my idea:

Love,

Here are some examples of TV-viewing rules that kindergartners suggested to their parents. The teacher created an open-ended worksheet to provide a structure for the children's work and included an introductory text in the form of a letter to parents. The children's rules provide a window into what they learned from discussions about TV rules. For instance, the child who wants the rule, No watching on sunny days, seems to realize that on nice days children should play outside instead of watching TV.

Meredith's rule

Alyssa's rule

Andrew's rule

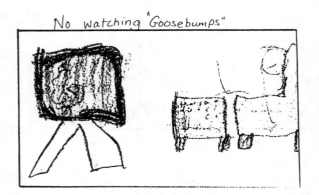

Greig's rule

April 7, 1997

Dear family

In school we have been learning about kids and TV. Now that it's Turn Off The TV Week, we're talking about the TV rules we have in our homes. I think we should have the following TV rules in our house:

1. no talking wen the t.v. is on.

2. no standing in front of the t.v.

3. no violent shows.

Let's talk about these ideas as a family so we can have TV rules we all agree on!

Love, Cory

Second graders wrote letters to their parents about TV rules. These letters (in contrast to the previous kindergarten letters) illustrate how activities suggested in this book can be adapted to be developmentally and academically appropriate to different groups of children.

April 7, 1997

Dear mom and Dad

In school we have been learning about kids and TV. Now that it's Turn Off The TV Week, we're talking about the TV rules we have in our homes. I think we should have the following TV rules in our house:

1. no soup operas

2. make a limit for T.V.

3. no woching moves the tor radid

Let's talk about these ideas as a family so we can have TV rules we all agree on!

Love, Kimberly

Help children reduce their dependence on television and other media.

A vital part of helping children successfully limit their viewing time is making sure they have appealing alternative activities. But do not be surprised to find that the more television children watch, the harder it may be for them to take charge of and limit their TV viewing.

It is not only what children see on TV that can create problems for them. TV time reduces children's opportunities to develop alternative interests or skills to use when they are not watching the screen. It also reduces opportunities to develop the kinds of skills needed to interact independently with the world in engaging and satisfying ways—such as through drawing, painting, exploring a special interest, or finding a wide variety of ways to play with a toy.

Help children reduce their screen time, especially their viewing of media violence, and consider appealing alternative activities. A key to achieving success here is helping children develop a range of activities, interests, and skills that capture their interest, meet their needs, and are inherently satisfying.

Children's books can provide an effective starting point for talking about TV-free activities. Read and discuss *Mouse TV,* by Matt Novak, which is about the anxiety a mouse family experiences when its TV set breaks down. (Several other appropriate books are listed and annotated in the Resources section.) The family discovers many creative and interesting ways to spend time together.

After reading the book to her class, one kindergarten teacher then helped the children make a list of all their suggestions about what the mice could do instead of watching TV. She wrote down *all* of their ideas (even if they did not exactly answer the question or did not contribute in an obvious way to the discussion).

The children said the mouse family could

- get it repaired
- fix it
- get a new TV
- go upstairs in their room and play a game
- exchange the TV
- read books
- eat fruit
- build things with a hammer
- play in the sandbox
- play Legos
- play basketball
- play soccer
- play on the swings
- ride bikes
- play with toys
- play with dolls
- draw a picture
- play with blocks

After making the list above, the kindergartners each drew a picture of his or her favorite idea. They then made a big book of ideas for their class library.

They could ride bikes.

*Four-year-olds drew what they thought the **Mouse TV family** could do after their TV broke. The teacher made all the children's drawings into a big book.*

DALYA

They could play with dolls.

• If you do not have a book like *Mouse TV*, start the discussion with "Pretend your TV set broke . . . ." Make a list or chart (with illustrations, especially for nonreaders) of children's ideas.

Kindergartners illustrated their ideas about what they could do if their TV set went on the blink, like it did in the Mouse TV *book.*

In <u>Mouse TV</u>, the mouse family had to find new things to do when their TV broke. Draw a picture of something you would do if your TV broke.

If my TV broke, I would play cop and robbers with my friend Andrew and my brother Joe

In <u>Mouse TV</u>, the mouse family had to find new things to do when their TV broke. Draw a picture of something you would do if your TV broke.

If my TV broke, I would play the card game "hearts"

In <u>Mouse TV</u>, the mouse family had to find new things to do when their TV broke. Draw a picture of something you would do if your TV broke.

If my TV broke, I would play rocket ship

- Post a Free-Time Activity Ideas chart in a central place in the classroom and add children's new activity ideas to it throughout the year. Send home copies of your Free-Time Activity Ideas so parents and children can talk about how to develop alternative activities. Ask parents to send in their own family's ideas for the list.

- Have a discussion on "What did you do over the weekend (or yesterday) besides watch TV?" Make a list. Ask children to brainstorm and add to the list other things they could have done.

During their school's special TV-Free Week, children made drawings of activities they could do instead of watching TV. To the teacher's surprise, many of the children simply turned to other forms of screen time, such as video games, videos, or computers.

Instead of watching T.V. I could play chess on the computer

Instead of watching T.V. I could make a video

Instead of watching T.V. I could play Gameboy.

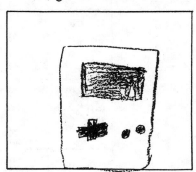

- Ask older children to keep a diary of what they do with their out-of-school time. Then have the children make simple graphs of what they found out.

- Set up a system for children to teach each other about their out-of-school activities. They can share their special skills or interests. Have a regularly designated time for sharing and make a sign-up sheet for volunteers.

A Children Teaching Children Sign-up Sheet was used as a way to help kindergartners learn new activities that would cut down on their TV time or video-game play. Simple illustrations were added so that both readers and nonreaders could understand the chart. Throughout the year, as children learned new things they wanted to share with others, activities were added to the chart.

CHILDREN TEACHING CHILDREN
Sign-up Sheet

THE TEACHER	I CAN TEACH:		I WANT TO LEARN IT
Melanie	Checkers		1._____ 2._____ 3._____
Jason	Bubble Blowing		1._____ 2._____ 3._____
Kathy	Hard puzzles		1._____ 2._____ 3._____
Julie & Michael	Lego marble ramps		1._____ 2._____ 3._____
Arthur	Drawing Action Figures		1._____ 2._____ 3._____
Henry	Stamp collecting		1._____ 2._____ 3._____
Amena	Cat's cradle		1._____ 2._____ 3._____

Help children learn how to reduce the impact of advertising on their consumer choices.

As we know, children—especially young children—are highly receptive to the advertising they see in the media.[31] Their thinking also makes it hard for them to understand how to resist advertising's influence. Still, there is a lot we can do to help children learn about resisting the lure of advertising and making informed consumer choices. Activities in the previous chapter that focus on advertising, the activities in Chapter 8 focusing on broken toys, as well as the activities that follow, will all reduce the effects of media advertising on children.

Talk with children about their responses to the commercials and product-linked programs they see in the media. One effective way to do this is to ask children if they have toys and other products that they saw advertised on TV. Then help the children compare the ad with their experience with the actual product.

Help children learn to make informed consumer decisions rather than rely on the lure of products they see in the media. Read *Arthur's TV Trouble,* by Marc Brown, and talk about your children's own experiences with wanting and getting things they saw on commercials. The book is about Arthur wanting a ridiculous product he sees advertised on TV. He saves the money to buy it but when he finally gets it, Arthur is disappointed. The toy is not at all like the ad promised.

ACTION IDEA

Ask the children if they ever have had an experience like Arthur's. Talk about what they think they learned from the experience and how they will try to do things differently the next time they see an appealing ad. Children also can make pictures of their experiences.

After reading Arthur's TV Trouble, children drew pictures of toys and other products that they had seen advertised on TV but that, after purchase, had disappointed them in one way or another. Here's how the teacher began the activity: "In Arthur's TV Trouble, Arthur bought a Treat Timer for Pal because of the commercials he had seen on TV. When Arthur brought the treat timer home from the store, he found that it didn't work like it did on the commercial. Have you ever had a toy that disappointed you because it wasn't like it seemed on TV? Tell about it. Draw a picture below."

"On the commercial Ballerina Barbie spins in circles, but I got her for Christmas and she doesn't spin."

"In the movie Toy Story, Buzz Lightyear's computer arm opened, but when I got it, the arm wouldn't open."

"On TV the bird tweeted, but in real life it didn't."

Fostering Creative Play to Counteract the Negative Impact of Media Culture

When 2-year-old Sasha plays with her favorite stuffed animal, Hoppi (that's hippo with the vowels switched), she often uses a very high-pitched voice. She shares everything with Hoppi—even snacks.

This morning Sasha asks her mother if she can turn on the TV. When her request is turned down, she makes a big frown and goes over to Hoppi. She asks him if he would like to see if "Thomas the Tank Engine" is on TV. She sits on the couch with Hoppi and watches the blank TV screen. She begins to give Hoppi a play-by-play account of her version of a *Winnie the Pooh* episode. "See, Hoppi? Don't you see Pooh flying? Do you see he wants some honey?" Soon she "switches channels" to *Sesame Street*. She now begins to explain counting; "Listen, Hoppi—1-2-3-4-5-6-7, like that. Can you count too? Can Big Bird help you count?"

The importance of play in development and learning

Play is vital to all aspects of children's healthy development and learning. Children actively use their play to master experience and skills and to try out new things. In the process they build new ideas and skills. They find interesting problems to work on, solve those problems in creative ways, and learn about the sense of power that can come from actively working out things on their own.

We see 2-year-old Sasha doing these things in her TV-watching play with Hoppi. When she encounters a problem—not being allowed to turn on the television—she figures out a meaningful and satisfying way to "watch" on her own. Her solution allows her to go over her prior experience with particular TV programs, using those parts that are most meaningful to her. Because she knows how to play on her own and create her own play, she is able to deal with the frustration of not being able to watch TV. In a deep sense, her play epitomizes the process of meaning-making described in earlier chapters, a process that is an essential part of all effective learning for young children—in this case, it is making meaning about TV.

The role of toys in play

The kinds of toys children use in their play can influence what and how they play. Some toys are likely to promote higher-quality play than others. Toys that are open-ended and unstructured, such as clay, blocks, generic toy figures and baby dolls, and even Hoppi, tend to encourage play that children shape in their own ways to meet their needs over time.

Single-purpose, highly structured, or realistic toys, like Batman or Star Wars action figures based on TV programs and/or movies, can have the opposite effect. They channel children into playing particular themes in particular ways. This affects not only how well children meet their needs in their play but also the lessons they learn from play.

The special problems media violence and media-linked toys create for children's play and learning[32]

Because of their level of development, young children can have a hard time dealing directly with the issues raised and problems created by violence in media and toys.[33] Instead, they often bring the violence they see to their play.

Media violence and media-linked toys create worrisome problems in two key areas. First, the nature and quality of the *play process* itself can be affected. Second, *what children learn* as they play can be affected.

A central role of play is to help children work out an understanding of their experience, including direct experience and the content they get from books, TV, and other media. The more children's play is a creation of their imagination, abilities, and needs, the more fully their social, emotional, and intellectual needs are met. In other words, when children—as scriptwriters, actors, prop people, producers, and directors—control what happens in their play, they are most likely to get the full benefits of play. And because children are unique individuals, bringing their unique experiences, abilities, needs, and understandings to their play, each child's play should be unique.

Much of the play resulting from children's exposure to the media involves children *imitating* the most salient aspects of what they have seen—often, the violence—rather than developing their own personally meaningful scripts and scenarios. Highly realistic toys that replicate media characters and paraphernalia tend to channel children into imitating what they have seen on the screen. And the combination of TV scripts and replica toys can make it really hard for children to develop their own personally meaningful play scenarios. Creative and imaginative play is replaced by imitative play.

When children lose control of their play—whether the content they are imitating is violent or not—one of their central avenues for growth and learning is undermined. When violence is added to the picture, the problem becomes even more worrisome.

Media violence and media-linked toys also influence the content of children's play. The content of play comes from what children are exposed to in daily life—including the media. Because the most popular children's TV programs, movies, and video games are violent and the toys linked to this media are also violent, children often have a real need to bring into their play the violent content they see in the media so they can make sense of it. But when they try to do so, the toys channel them into imitating the violence they see on the screen. And then the toys help to keep children riveted on that violent focus. In this way, media-linked toys become a primary vehicle through which children use their imitative play to learn the lessons about violence they see on the screen.

Because they get stuck just imitating what they have seen, children often cannot work through the violent content that they need to in their play. In addition, the whole range of meaningful content from children's experience, which should be central to their play, can be severely shortchanged. But of even greater concern is what children learn about violence as they experience the apparent fun, excitement, and power that their violent actions seem to bring to human interactions and conflicts.

Here is one teacher's account of the contrast she noticed in play themes and toys that were and were not linked to the media. It illustrates many of the issues identified above.

I teach a morning and afternoon class of 4- and 5-year-olds. In one class I have boys who are very influenced by media. Early in the year they focused a lot on *Toy Story* and those characters and a smattering of Power Rangers. Then several boys saw *Star Wars* at the movies. They brought Star Wars merchandise catalogs to look at during library time. At the art table they try to draw Darth Vader, Luke Skywalker, and other characters. A child brought in a Star Wars comic book. Another wanted to "write" a Star Wars story. After one boy went to Disney World, he talked constantly about meeting Darth Vader, having his picture taken with Star Wars characters, and seeing Star Wars shows. Now he wants to wear only white clothes like Han Solo.

The boys have been playing Star Wars endlessly—building spaceships and shooting lasers, talking about the Star Wars "good guys" and "bad guys." It comes up in their discussions over and over and over again.

Interestingly, the girls have not shown much interest in this topic. They have become more separated from the boys' dramatic play since Star Wars took over.

The dramatic play is *very* different in my other class. It has centered all year around Beanie Babies. Girls and boys have brought them in and played together building play themes around them. I've been thrilled. There's no TV show to influence their play (yet), so they spend hours in the block corner building Beanie Baby houses and using their imaginations on all kinds of play in the houses. They've also come up with other Beanie Baby play themes.

WHAT YOU CAN DO

Sasha's play with Hoppi is an example of the kind of play to aim for. What she does is her own unique creation—she works on her own issues in her own ways to build her own meanings and find solutions. You can help all children develop this kind of play to work through their salient experiences, including the media they see.

Observe children as they play and use the information you collect as a basis for deciding how to facilitate their play.

Look for such information as

- individual play abilities, styles, and interests

- the content that seems to most interest individual children

- media content that comes up in play (How is it imitative of scripts and how is it creative play of the children's own design?)

- toys that are the most or least appealing and with which the children are the most and least comfortable

- problems that come up in play (When do various children run into trouble with their play? with other children?)

- areas in which children seem to need the most help in expanding and developing their play

*Encourage children to play with toys that they can use
in many ways rather than play with highly realistic,
media-linked toys that dictate what and how to play.*

Becoming skillful at using a *few* open-ended toys (such as blocks, play-dough, and dress-up clothes) in many different ways can lead children to more productive play in the long run. But with open-ended toys, some children still need help in developing skill and finding interesting problems to work on. For children who have trouble playing with open-ended toys, somewhat realistic toys—those that suggest ideas for play but are not linked to media actions and scripts—can provide an extra impetus.

Use the following Toy Selection Guide when evaluating and choosing toys and other play materials for your children. You also can use it when buying a gift for an individual child.

Toy Selection Guide	
Choose toys that	*Avoid toys that*
can be used in a variety of ways	can only be used in one way
promote creativity and problem solving because they let children decide how they will be used	encourage everyone to play the same way and work on problems defined by the toy designer
can be enjoyed at different ages and stages	appeal primarily to children of a single age or developmental stage
continue to be fun and engaging over time	sit on a shelf after the first 10 minutes of fun
can be used with other toys to create new and more complex play opportunities	channel children into imitating the violent scripts they see in the media
promote respectful, nonstereo-typical, nonviolent interactions among children	encourage violence and stereotypes that lead to disrespectful, aggressive interactions

Examples of toys to buy
• blocks • modeling clay and playdough • construction sets (Legos, Toobers & Zots, etc.) • culturally diverse dolls • trucks and trains • balls • puzzles

Help children find compelling play content or scripts that grow out of their own meaningful experiences and interests.

This encourages children to move away from the highly imitative, violent, and repetitive play that comes from the media. When teachers help children add new and personally meaningful content to their media-linked play (for instance, set up a restaurant like the teacher suggested for the children who played Power Rangers), play can quickly become more creative. In some cases, teachers report, children move totally away from TV-influenced play.

Activities such as creating a pet store, fire station, spaceship, restaurant, or hospital offer children lots of possibilities for dramatization of meaningful content. Props like those listed on pp. 85—86 in the Shoe Box Kit Ideas can get you started gathering materials for such play.

ACTION IDEA

Use children's books to provide children with play ideas and themes. The Resources section of this book lists a few particularly appealing books. After reading a book, help children create props that focus play on central aspects of the story.

Create and equip environments that help children start and sustain meaningful play.

Well-organized and well-equipped settings can help children find interesting ways to get started and then stay involved. A child can easily get distracted from play while going in search of a certain prop. Help children learn to find and use materials independently. For instance, organize toys in ways that children understand and have easy access to. Keeping playthings in labeled containers with simple picture labels helps children find things they need. This also aids cleanup.

Choose materials for play carefully. Materials should suggest but not control what children do. Too many play items can distract children and promote superficial involvement. When children get interested in a particular kind of play or theme, group together materials that might further develop the play.

Gather materials and props that promote play around themes you think will interest your children.

The following list of shoe box kits provides some ideas to help you get started. Copy and distribute the list to parents and teachers. They might want to consider giving a shoe box kit as an alternative to a commercially bought gift.

Shoe Box Kit Ideas

Children's toys do not have to be manufactured. Shoe box kits are collections of small, familiar items organized around a play theme, conveniently put together, and presented in an appealing way.

When carefully chosen to fit the interests of a child, shoe box kits provide hours of creative and satisfying play that individual children can adapt and shape to meet their own skill and interest levels. They also help children learn that expensive, fancy-packaged toys aren't the only good gifts—that common household objects put together in interesting ways often provide more long-lasting fun.

The process of putting together such an easy, yet imaginative, kit for a special child in your life can be very satisfying for you too. It makes a great gift.

Guidelines for making shoe box kits

- Start with an empty shoe box (or any box with a lid).

- Cover the box with paper and decorate it.

- Choose a theme that fits the interests of the child you have in mind. (Some ideas for themes are listed on the following page.)

- Put on the box a clear label that identifies the theme with both a simple word and picture. Even very young children will enjoy "reading" the label.

- Have fun choosing from the list of theme ideas. Or use it as a jumping off point to add things you come up with. Or create your own themes.

- Most of the suggested items can be found at hardware stores, pharmacies, stationary stores, and art/crafts stores.

- Be selective—you don't need to include everything listed to create a wonderful kit.

- Use small containers, zippered sandwich bags, or dividers made with small pieces of cardboard to make compartments for the various items in the shoe box. Young children appreciate organization, being able to return everything to its place.

- Most of these suggestions are appropriate and safe for children to use independently; however, objects in some kits may require adult supervision and/or aid (e.g., with food coloring).

- Once children begin using the box, be on the lookout for things to replenish and add to the box. Encourage children to add to it too.

Shoe Box Kit Theme Ideas*

Baby
(to use with a doll or stuffed animal)
- newborn disposable diapers
- empty plastic baby food jars
- baby-size spoon
- plastic baby bottle
- bibs
- infant clothes
- baby blanket
- washcloth
- pacifier
- rattle

Bath and Water Play
- spray bottle
- squirt bottle
- soap crayons
- eggbeater
- bubble wands
- plastic animals
- plastic nesting cups
- sponges/fancy washcloths
- plastic colander
- turkey baster
- plastic eyedroppers
- clear plastic tubing

Detective
- magnifying glass (plastic lens)
- small notepad and pen
- handcuffs
- maps
- tie-ons/sticky labels (to label clues)
- clear plastic containers (to store evidence in)
- ink pad/paper (for fingerprinting)

Office
- stapler (4 or 5 years & up)
- hole puncher
- tape
- sticky labels or message pad
- small clipboard
- receipt book
- blank labels
- key ring with old keys
- pens/pencils/markers
- carbon paper
- ink pad & stamps

Playdough
- buy basic playdough colors or make your own dough (see recipe below)
- garlic press
- plastic knives
- popsicle sticks
- wooden dowel
- plastic lids
- small tray/plate
- buttons/beads
- Styrofoam packing material
- miniature plastic animals

Recipe for Playdough
2 c. flour
1 c. salt
1 T. cream of tartar
2 c. water colored with food coloring
1 T. vegetable oil

Mix and cook over medium heat, stirring constantly. Remove from heat when mixture looks like thick mashed potatoes. When cool enough to touch, knead it. Store in plastic container with lid or in a zip bag.

Rescue/First Aid
- flashlight
- Band-Aids
- ace bandage
- sling
- eye patch
- gauze
- stethoscope
- surgical mask

Stringing
- fishing line or plastic cord
- yarn with tape at ends
- Styrofoam shapes
- washers/nuts
- old thread spools
- buttons
- plastic or wooden beads

*Some of these kits contain items that are too small for younger children. When choosing the items to put in a kit, make sure you keep in mind the age of the children.

***Try to develop an approach to media-linked war play
that responds to the needs of children as well as your own
concerns and goals for the children.***

Many teachers and parents would like to ban media-linked war play and toys from their children's lives. This is totally understandable. But merely banning violent content does not really address the problems created by media violence and toys.

Banning such play often just pushes the issues underground. It does not give children a chance to work through their feelings about and experiences with media violence. It also cuts off adults from influencing how children process the violent content they see and what they learn from it. For these reasons, it is important to find safe ways to help children work through the violent content they see in the media. For young children, this usually means in their play.

The box on p. 88 provides guidelines for developing an approach to the media-linked war-play dilemma.

ACTION IDEAS

Observe and talk to children as they engage in play with violence. This will help you to learn more about what they know and think so you are in a better position to determine if and how their play is imitative or creative. You also can gather the information you need to decide if, when, and how to intervene.

Make give-and-take discussions about issues of play, toys, and violence a regular part of any approach you take with children. The discussion in Chapter 2 about Henry's understanding of the Star Wars movie, the problem-solving discussion in Chapter 4 about the Power Rangers, and the parent-child dialogue in Chapter 10 about how much TV to watch provide examples to help you begin. So does the letter to parents about gender roles and toys at the end of this chapter.

Finding an Approach to Media-Linked Play with Violence

Any effective approach for dealing with war play

- *ensures the safety of all children*

   Children often need lots of help learning how to play in ways that keep themselves and others safe.

- *promotes development of imaginative and creative play (rather than imitative play)*

   Whatever content children bring to their play, they should have an opportunity to work it out, learn healthy lessons, and move on to new issues.

- *tries to reduce dependence on highly realistic, media-linked "fighting" toys*

   This can help reduce the external pull to engage in imitative war play and get stuck there.

- *promotes use of open-ended toys*

   Children themselves can control how these toys are used rather than being controlled by a toy.

- *provides opportunities to work out an understanding of the media violence children see and hear*

   When children are exposed to violence they need acceptable channels to deal with it, whether in play or through some other avenue like drawing or talking.

- *helps to counteract the violence lessons that children are learning*

   As children reveal what they know and think, you can use ideas presented throughout this book, such as give-and-take discussions and conflict-resolution strategies, to counteract the negative lessons.

- *involves children in decisionmaking*

   The more children can participate in decisionmaking about if and how they engage in play with violence, the more they will understand, accept, and learn.

- *evolves as circumstances and needs of children and groups change*

   Children's needs are unique and change rapidly, as do the media and toy culture.

- *connects home and school*

   Because media violence so permeates children's play culture, teachers and parents need to work together to deal with and reduce its effects.

- *limits and minimizes effects of exposure to violent play content as much as possible*

   Because there will be less troubling content to work out, children will have less need to bring violence issues into their play.

Work to counteract the stereotypes that are often found in media-linked toys and play.

Many of the most popular media-linked toys are highly gender stereotyped. You can tell whether most toys at mass market toy stores are for girls or for boys merely by looking at the colors of the toy boxes. Too many of these toys provide a very narrow definition of what boys and girls do—generally the most extreme and distinct behaviors, with boys being tough, often brutal, and girls being pretty and sweet.

Furthermore, there is an increase in the quantity and quality of sexual imagery in these toys—for instance, female figures increasingly have exaggerated breasts and revealing clothing. Much of what children see in these toys is constantly reinforced by what they see in popular TV shows, movies, and video games.

Sexual imagery, a close-up view.

Cosmic Angela™

Here are examples of illustrations on boxes for media-linked toys that have gender stereotyped and sexualized appearance. Baywatch Barbie, for children over 3, is based in the TV show Baywatch. The box suggests that children can "play real lifeguard adventures with Barbie like you see on the hot TV show!" She-Spawn, an action figure in the Spawn toy line, is based on the popular comic book and newly released movie. She-Spawn has carved skulls on her exaggerated breasts.

The following captions, taken from a random assortment of action figure and doll boxes on a toy store's shelves, graphically illustrate the broad divisions and extreme behaviors promoted by toys for boys and girls.

Captions on Toy Packages for Dolls and Action Figures

Baby Wiggles N' Giggles—"Tickle my bow—I wiggle and giggle."

Ghost Rider—"Wind up his arm to activate the whip."

Katy Kiss & Giggle—"I give pretty pink lipstick kisses . . . I make kissing sounds, giggle, and say 'I love you.'"

Aliens Vs. Predator Clan Leader— "With whipping dread-locks and power boots."

Original Tattle Talk Friends—"I say everything you say."

Smart Sharks—"Open and close piranha masks for real biting power."

Sweet Angels—"Hug me and I sing 'This Little Light of Mine' and my halo lights up."

Stone Protectors—"Cellular mow phone with megamulcher mower blade and day/night assault weapon. You can dim the daylights out of devilish desperadoes."

Help boys and girls play together as well as develop a wide repertoire of acceptable behaviors for their gender. The more open-ended children's toys are and the less media-linked content children bring to their play, the more common ground girls and boys will find for their play. Use the give-and-take approach to discussions about gender issues in toys, media, and play.

ACTION IDEA

Look at toy boxes with children. Younger children can just look at the pictures. Older children can talk about the pictures and words and discuss the kinds of behaviors and stereotypes that are promoted. Ask such questions as "What does the picture tell you about this toy?" "What kinds of things does this toy do that boys/girls really do or do not do?" If it is a "girls' toy," ask the children if they think that boys can play with it (and vice versa) and why or why not?

The following letter to parents, written by a teacher of a combined kindergarten-first grade, describes a discussion about gender stereotypes and toys. It grew unexpectedly out of a curriculum unit on the five senses.

Letter to Parents about What's Happening in Our Classroom

Dear Parents:

The classroom continues to be a busy place. It's exciting to watch the group at this point in the year. They're comfortable with each other, with the routines, with the expectations, and with themselves. When we work together now on projects, the children come up with such interesting information and ideas. Here's an example of one discussion that illustrates how things are going.

In studying the five senses, we began talking about how eyes and ears work. We planned a visit by a physician to help us understand these parts of our body. In preparation, I put out some books about the senses for children to look at. One book thoughtfully raises the issue of gender roles and discusses similarities and differences between boys and girls. It challenges stereotypes about length of hair, style of clothes, kinds of toys or games, emotions, and sports.

As we read the book, giggles erupted when I read the page, "Some people think only girls play with dolls, but Noah's a boy and he likes to take care of his dolls." A lengthy conversation ensued about whether boys play with dolls, what's the difference between action figures (mostly from TV) and dolls, what about stuffed animals, and who decides how a toy is used. The children were full of opinions and ideas. In fact, the conversation lasted over the course of three days. The conversation among the children was amazing. We'd like to share a few pieces of the dialogue with you:

"I used to think dolls were only for girls, but then I went to M's house and he had a doll, so I changed my mind. Right, M?"

A few boys said, "I'm [my brother's] a boy and I [he] play[s] with dolls." And more than one girl offered, "Well, I'm a girl and I hate dolls."

(continued on next page)

"Dolls are for girls and action figures are for boys," one boy declared. When pressed a bit further about how they were different, the child responded, "With action figures you have fights and battles—you know, it's a war. And with dolls, you feed and dress them and put them in bed. You know, dolls are about living." When asked if action figures need to eat, he replied, "No, it's just about war."

Another boy forcefully disagreed. "GI Joe eats and sleeps. He has to or else he wouldn't be GI Joe."

One child noted, "It's commercials that try to make you think toys are just for either boys or girls. They try to trick you into thinking that so you'll buy them."

"You're the one who decides how to play with a toy. You can make Barbies fight just as much as you can make action figures fight. No one or no thing can tell you how to play with a toy."

"You watch TV. That tells you how to use a figure and what they should do. Sometimes it tells you on the back of the box."

"The difference between action figures and dolls is that action figures always look the same, and you can change the way dolls look by changing their clothes."

"Stuffed animals and trolls are like dolls or figures. You can play with them in a lot of ways."

"Playing with dolls or figures does not decide whether or not you're a boy or a girl."

We were impressed with how articulate and thoughtful the children were and how understanding and tolerant they tried to be of each other's feelings and opinions. This idea of feeling safe enough to express your feelings even if it isn't the popular opinion was a very important part of this experience.

We hope you enjoyed hearing about this special experience your children had. We welcome hearing from you about it and will keep you informed of new developments.

Help children look at other prevalent stereotypes that are reinforced by media-linked toys. In addition to these gender stereotypes in media and media-linked toys, children see many other stereotypes about such things as race, economic class, nationality, who is good and bad, and who are friends and enemies. This type of stereotyping is bad for children. It undermines their opportunities both in and out of play to develop to their full potential as girls and boys. It also can undermine children's gradually developing ability to appreciate and respect similarities and differences among people and avoid stereotypical thinking.

When Pretend Meets Real—
Responding to Violence in the News

Media-reported violence often intrudes on daily classroom life in unexpected ways. For example, in the winter of 1997, a kindergartner abruptly brought up the murder of Ennis Cosby. Her teacher was taken off-guard. She recalls,

> I don't usually regard my students as being affected by issues of violence. My thoughts about this, however, are changing. Recently, the high-profile murders of 5-year-old JonBenet Ramsey and Bill Cosby's son, Ennis, dominated talk shows, TV news, newspapers, and radio. I know these tragedies dominated the conversations in staff lounges, but I hadn't thought much about how young children might be processing the stories they've overheard.
>
> A few days after Ennis Cosby's murder, Kara, one of my students, said to me, "Ms. P, did you know Bill Cosby's son was killed on the highway?"
>
> I was completely dumbfounded and had no idea how to respond. Sometimes a teacher is faced with situations that seem like there's no way to win. I didn't feel comfortable discussing the murder with Kara in front of the other children. I was worried that some of the children hadn't heard about it, and I didn't want to expose them. I was concerned that some of the children would tell their parents, "In school today we talked about Bill Cosby's son getting killed." I imagined parents calling the school to express their anger that the teacher talked about nonschool-related things.
>
> On the other hand, Kara obviously wanted to talk about what she knew had happened. I didn't really know what I should say to her. I wasn't sure why she had told me. Did she simply want to be the first to share a gruesome tale? Did she have questions about the murder? Was she worried?

Some adults appear unaware that young children pay attention to or think about the violence they hear about on the news. But reports of violence are so prevalent both in our home and in out-of-home settings—on the TV and radio news and talk shows, in front-page newspaper headlines and photographs, on TV monitors in public places such as airport and physician waiting rooms, at friends' or relatives' houses, and in everyday conversation—that even when we try hard to protect children from real-world violence reported in the media, some will inevitably get through. And as technology becomes a greater and greater presence in children's lives, children cannot help but be exposed to more accounts of violence. We must accept the fact that children cannot be fully protected from the violence in the news.[34]

As the teacher's account above makes very clear, deciding what the adult's role should be in helping children deal with the real violence they are exposed to in the media presents a big challenge. Few adults, including teachers, receive training about how to deal with these issues. And few resources are available to help us figure out what to do either when children raise these issues spontaneously or when the situation allows a more planned and intentional response.[35]

Understandably, most of us would prefer to avoid having to deal with these issues. There are many reasons why. We never can be sure what a child might say or where such conversations might lead—a scary thought with such potentially scary content! We also want to protect children from the evils in the world—protect their innocence—as long as possible. We worry about saying the wrong thing, something that might add to rather than relieve a child's worries. We want to lessen the evil the child hears about, yet we are usually powerless to do so. We worry about how other adults, especially parents, will react to what we do. The teacher in the above example voices many of these issues in the split second she has to try to figure out how to respond to Kara.

Yet when we do not deal with violence in the news with children, we are abrogating our responsibility to help children sort out what they hear and to figure out what it means. We are teaching children not to talk to the important adults in their lives about disturbing issues. We are leaving them to deal with the violence on their own, without guidance, reassurance, and support. We are giving up the opportunity to influence the lessons they learn from what they hear. We are not helping them sort out what is pretend and what is real in the media and in real life, or to deal with concerns that may arise—for instance, about their own safety. And we are not helping them develop concepts and a language for dealing with what they hear.

A special word about children who directly experience violence

The degree to which children are exposed to violence varies greatly, as does the degree to which they are affected. Many children directly experience violence in their own lives, rather than just hear about it in the media. The ideas children build about the role of violence in human interactions come from all of their exposures to violence; children who experience it directly, as well as through the media, use what they learn about violence from both kinds of experiences to build their ideas about violence. In fact, experience with real violence is likely to alter—and often intensify—children's reaction to media violence.

The following figure places the kinds of violence in children's lives along a continuum. It provides a way of thinking about the cumulative effects of violence on children. At the bottom of the continuum is entertainment violence (which is most prevalent in society and touches most children's lives). Next comes violence children hear about in the news. And at the top are the most extreme forms of violence—chronic and direct exposure in the immediate environment (which fewer children experience but which builds onto the exposure to the other forms of violence below it on the pyramid). The degree to which children are affected by violence is likely to increase as they move up the continuum.

It is beyond the scope of this book to fully address this issue. However, the suggestions in this chapter can provide the necessary foundation and starting points for your efforts to help children deal with the range of ways violence enters their lives.

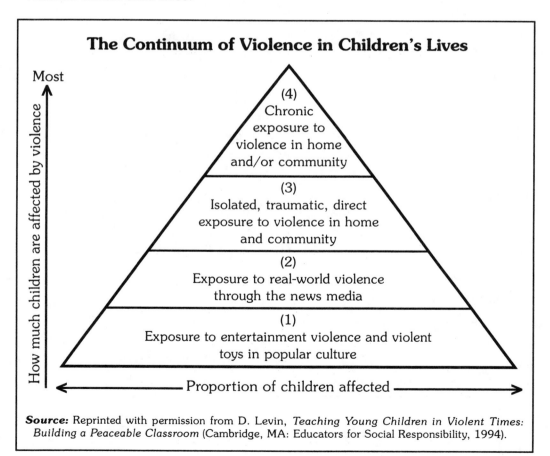

The Continuum of Violence in Children's Lives

Most

How much children are affected by violence

(4)
Chronic exposure to violence in home and/or community

(3)
Isolated, traumatic, direct exposure to violence in home and community

(2)
Exposure to real-world violence through the news media

(1)
Exposure to entertainment violence and violent toys in popular culture

← Proportion of children affected →

Source: Reprinted with permission from D. Levin, *Teaching Young Children in Violent Times: Building a Peaceable Classroom* (Cambridge, MA: Educators for Social Responsibility, 1994).

WHAT YOU CAN DO

Learn how to help children deal with the real-world violence they hear about on the news.

Realizing the importance of addressing media violence issues with children is one thing. Knowing how to do it is another! The kindergarten teacher, in her struggle to figure out how to respond to Kara's question, grapples with several of the complexities involved in addressing issues of real-world violence in the news and children's needs. The commentary accompanying the teacher's following account highlights these complexities.

The Dilemma	Commentary
There were no easy answers to Kara's question; I couldn't give it a happy ending. Even though I wanted to, I knew I couldn't just make the question go away. She brought it to me for a reason and I had to respect that.	By raising the issue this way Kara shows she wants/needs to talk about it and that she feels safe doing so with her teacher. Children quickly learn where they can and cannot talk about these things.
I said, "Yes, Kara, I did hear about that story. It made me very sad. Tell me what you heard."	After a brief personal reaction, the teacher focuses on finding out more about what Kara knows and wants to talk about. This lets Kara know that asking the question is okay and that the teacher wants to hear her ideas.
She quickly reviewed the details she knew: "Ennis was driving his car and he got a flat tire. He got out of his car, and someone shot him and then drove away, and the police didn't catch him."	Without intervening, the teacher lets Kara talk about what she knows. Often this is all that a child wants and needs.
Again I was surprised at all the information Kara had and I was unsure of what to do next.	At each step of this discussion, the teacher must decide how to respond based on what she learns from Kara.

The Dilemma	Commentary
Other children now were coming over to listen to our conversation. They were becoming curious about the story. Nancy asked, "What happened?" I felt in over my head.	Once a child begins talking, others may overhear. One big challenge of dealing with hard issues in a classroom is figuring out what to do with children's different levels of exposure and knowledge, as well as parents' diverse opinions about how to deal with such issues.
Thankfully (I think), Kara chimed in to restate the story for Nancy.	Children, on their own, often do a good job responding to each other's questions and concerns.
Nancy seemed uninterested, but Kara kept spouting details. Her story was accurate from the reports I had heard. She wasn't asking me questions and didn't seem to be troubled by the incident. She simply rambled on and on about the tragedy in the way she often talks about what her family did the night before or about a children's TV program she watched. Then she walked away.	Children have their own unique reactions, and the teacher uses this information to guide her response. Nancy gets an answer and is ready to move on. Kara needs to go over the details of the case, and the teacher is there to listen.

Young children often do not differentiate between fictional and real violence they see on the screen. |
A few minutes later, I went over to the art table where Kara was working. She blurted out that her dad once had a flat tire. She pointed to her paper, which had a big black donut shape drawn on it, and said, "Here's the tire."	Kara seems to be connecting what she heard about Ennis Cosby's murder to her own experience with her family's flat tire. Children often relate what they hear in the news to their own direct experience.
At first, I reacted to her picture matter-of-factly. Then a light bulb went off. I realized that she probably was connecting her dad's flat tire to what she had heard about Ennis Cosby and that she might need some help working this out.	Children often continue to work out their ideas about what they have heard over a period of time—often in their art or play. It is important for adults to keep on the lookout to see what comes up and how things evolve.
I asked Kara questions to try to find out more. They were on their way to visit her grandmother. Her father changed the tire himself. Kara watched.	Here again, before jumping in with a response, an adult should try to find out what the child knows and use that information in shaping a response.

(continued on next page)

The Dilemma	Commentary
Then I tried to reassure her with factual information by saying, "You know, a lot of people have flat tires. That's why cars have spares and those jacks so people can lift the car up to put on new tires and then safely go where they need to go. Your dad knew just what to do so he could fix it, and then you all could still go to your grammy's."	Using the information Kara provided, the teacher focuses on her father's ability to keep her safe.
	By not making a direct connection between the flat tire in the Cosby murder and the family's flat tire, the teacher is focusing on the information she thinks will be most useful to Kara—that she is safe and that her father knows how to keep her safe. Children often focus on their own issues and concerns—their own safety and experience—and do not need all the information about a situation that an adult might require.
I'm not sure I handled the entire situation in the best way possible.	There is rarely a "best" way to deal with these issues, nor is this teacher's response the only possible appropriate one. Every teacher and group of children shape their own give-and-take discussion as it goes along, seeing where it leads.
My thoughts were that I should just be an ear to listen, and if Kara needed clarification, I may be able to provide that. If she needed comforting I could provide that. If she needed reassurance for her own safety, I could fill that need too. Initially, it seemed that she just wanted to talk about the events, not her feelings or the impact it was having on her, the Cosby family, or anyone else. When she told me about her experience with the flat tire, it seemed like she was comparing her experience to what she had heard. Then I did need to reassure her.	This teacher knows there are several different factors to keep in mind when deciding on a response. She realizes she must shape and adapt her response as the situation evolves.
	Children often need reassurance about their own safety when they hear scary things in the news. Kara does not seem to need it at the beginning, but later this need starts to emerge.
	The teacher sees that while Kara can describe the Cosby tragedy in a logical manner, she is still thinking differently about it than adults would. Kara chooses a few salient issues to focus on, not the whole context or more far-reaching implications, and the focus of the issues changes over time.
	The same general characteristics of young children's thinking described in Chapter 2 also shape how children interpret what they hear in the news.

The Dilemma	Commentary
I've now become comfortable discussing media violence with children in ways that challenge their thinking about pretend violence. True violence, however, is much more of a challenge to discuss. I know parents often want to reassure their young children that the violence they see on TV is not real and reassure their children that they are safe. I think safety is a crucial place to start, but I have concerns about oversimplifying violence by only saying that it isn't real.	This kind of reflection, after the episode with Kara ended, is an important part of the process of helping children deal with issues of violence that come up in the classroom. It can help teachers reflect on what they have learned about the children and figure out if they should do any follow-up work. It can point them in new directions. When possible, teachers should try to find other caring adults to share in this process.
My experience with pretend media violence is that it still greatly affects young children even though it isn't real. The Cosby and Ramsey cases complicate things further for children because they've been on TV where children often view pretend violence, but this time the violence they saw on TV really happened. How do I help children reconcile the fun and exciting entertainment media violence with the real pain and suffering of the real-world violence that permeates our society?	Children rarely make neat and tidy distinctions about what in the media is pretend and what is real—news violence often gets clumped together with entertainment violence (as with the child in Chapter 2 who thought the Power Rangers needed to go fight in Haiti). While some children will become worried about their safety, other children will not react with the same distress to a real story that their peers or adults might. At the same time, because of the blurring of pretend and real violence, children also can experience the kinds of distress over entertainment violence that adults associate with real violence. That's one reason why adults need to explore children's meanings before deciding on an appropriate approach.

ACTION IDEA

Use this teacher's account as a starting point for beginning discussions with other adults about how to deal with similar issues with children. Getting input and support from others is one of the best ways to develop understanding and skill at helping children cope with the violence they hear about in the news.

Provide children with a variety of media for expressing and working out their ideas about violence reported in the news.

As is often the case, Kara dealt with what she heard about the Cosby tragedy by raising the subject with an adult. But words of assurance sometimes are not enough. And children do not always directly raise their concern with words. Many young children need more concrete ways to express and work out what they hear and what troubles them. Children often use painting, drawing, and other expressive art activities to work out violence issues. Kara used this technique when she made a picture of her family's flat tire.

Here is a 4-year-old's drawing of the bombing of the federal building in Oklahoma City in 1995. Just one of the many pictures he drew in the days after the bombing, it includes such details as blood, the cracks in the building, an ambulance taking injured people to the hospital, and helicopters rescuing people.

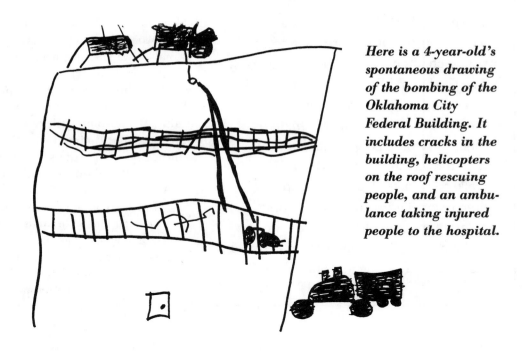

Here is a 4-year-old's spontaneous drawing of the bombing of the Oklahoma City Federal Building. It includes cracks in the building, helicopters on the roof rescuing people, and an ambulance taking injured people to the hospital.

As discussed in the last chapter, dramatic play is probably the most common and powerful avenue young children use to work out an understanding of their experience—and this holds true with the violence they are exposed to in the news. For instance, after the tragedy in Oklahoma City, many parents and teachers reported dramatic play that imitated the bombing: children demolished block buildings with accompanying boom-and-crash sound effects, pretended to be dead victims, rushed injured classmates to the hospital. This kind of reenactment, often recognized as a central part of play therapy for emotionally troubled children, illustrates the healing quality of play (without the need for therapy). Many young children spontaneously create play scenarios to deal with troubling information or events.

Here is the dramatic play that emerged at a child care center in Tennessee soon after the bombing in Oklahoma City. We can see how the teachers supported the children's efforts to make sense of the tragedy. (Guidelines for helping children deal with violence they hear about in the news appear at the end of this chapter.)

A group of 3- and 4-year-olds were playing in the block center, building a very large structure. Listening to their conversation, the staff soon realized the children were duplicating the Oklahoma City Federal Building that was bombed.

Continuing their play, the children destroyed the building and soon began to rescue one another. They assumed roles of doctors, firefighters, and police officers and tenderly began caring for those who were hurt. This play continued for some time as the children reconstructed their knowledge of the event and worked through their feelings about the incident.

Later the children also took the role of dogs searching for injured children. The children organized in groups of four to carry other children to safely. There were two brothers in the class. Another child called for one of the brothers: "Come quickly! He's your brother, and he's hurt."

Teachers observing this elaborate dramatic play were moved to tears. It was obvious that the children had been exposed to television coverage, bringing into their play many of the small details they had absorbed. Gradually, the children began to assign teachers roles, like being the doctor taking care of the wounded (children). And the teachers followed the children's lead.

One little girl made a connection between the Oklahoma City explosion and an army ammunition plant located near our school. She must have heard a conversation about the devastation that would occur if there were an explosion at this plant, and she began talking about how our school could blow up too. A teacher who heard this talked to her about the safety of the center and took her to the main office to see the special automated system connected to the police and fire department. Her face showed visible relief when she heard about how the equipment protected everybody.

This play and conversation continued for several days. Since firefighters, doctors, and police were such an important part of the children's play, the teachers planned a unit on Community Helpers to enhance the children's awareness of the city's emergency agencies. On a field trip we drove around town pointing out the Red Cross office, hospitals, fire stations, police station, army reserve headquarters, rescue squads, and more. The children drew their own maps as we traveled. We did not go inside any of

Children use dramatic play in the block area to work out an understanding of what they have heard about the Oklahoma City bombing.

these facilities because our focus was on helping the children see, quickly and concretely, all the ways their community keeps them safe and on helping them to feel safe in their community.

Most of our children are exposed to at least one violent act a day, either on TV or in their own lives. It is so important to give them the time to work through their anxieties, through play and conversation, and for teachers to be facilitators, resource people, *and,* most of all, caring adults.

Whatever medium children use to work on violence issues, we should recognize their efforts; learn as much as we can about what each child knows, understands, and is working on; and think about the roles we might play in assisting children with their efforts.

In your classroom routine, try to create regular avenues that children, especially older children, can use to raise issues they want to discuss.

One approach several teachers have told me works quite well is setting aside a regular time (such as once a week at the regular class meeting) when they ask the children, "Has anyone heard about anything in the news they would like to talk about?"[36] Of course, we never can be sure what issues might come up. But most of the time children will raise questions about such topics as sports and the weather (which are of value too). When more serious topics do surface, we should try to use an approach similar to that employed by Kara's teacher. The guidelines at the end of this chapter summarize some of the most important issues to keep in mind.

Help parents learn more about how to deal with the violence their children hear about in the news.

Work with parents to help them limit their child's exposure to violence in the news and help them develop strategies for dealing with the violence-laden news that does get through. Also keep parents informed about any troubling news item that comes up in your setting, how you are dealing with it, and what they might do.

Use class newsletters, parents' evenings, parent-teacher conferences, and notes or phone calls to home as opportunities to let parents know about issues that come up. In addition to giving parents information that will help them keep track of what is happening with their children, these vehicles provide a way to demonstrate classroom approaches to these issues and to present ideas about how families might respond.

Here is how one kindergarten teacher proceeded after she became concerned about the effects extensive exposure to TV news was having on a child.

Tommy came in one day and asked, "Ms. G, did you hear about the homicide in Boston last night?" This was the third time in a few days that Tommy had mentioned a news story like this to me, and I was beginning to become a bit concerned. I decided it was time to explore why he was bringing in so many news stories. So, after asking him to tell me what he knew about the murder, the discussion went in the following direction:

Teacher: Tommy, where did you hear about the "homicide"?

Tommy: I saw it on the *News at Six*.

Teacher: You watch the news when you get home?

Tommy: Yes, I watch it every night while my mom makes dinner.

Teacher: Sounds like you hear about scary things on the news.

Tommy: No. I'm used to it.[37]

The next week, during a regularly scheduled conference with Tommy's parents, I recounted his comment about the Boston murder. I mentioned that he often told me about things he had heard on the evening news and that I wondered what all he was hearing might mean to him.

Tommy's father said, "Maybe we shouldn't let him watch so much news." The mother nodded in agreement. After a bit more discussion, I asked them if they had ideas about how they would talk to Tommy about reducing his news time. We talked about positive ways to work on the issue with him.

As you develop your approach to working with children on issues of real-world violence in the media, keep in mind the following points.

Guidelines for Helping Children Deal with Violence in the News

- Trusted adults play a vital role in helping children sort out what they have heard and need to figure out. Let children know it is okay to raise these kinds of issues with you. Older children often benefit from a regular time built into the school week when they can raise and talk about these issues.

- Don't expect young children to understand violence as adults do. When you work on these issues with children, try to find out as much as you can about what each individual child knows and understands or is struggling to understand. Then base your responses on what you find out.

- When children hear about something scary or disturbing, they sometimes relate it to themselves and start to worry about their own safety. Even when you cannot make a situation better, reassure children about their safety—for instance, say, "That can't happen to you because your parents always___" This kind of reassurance is what children most need to hear.

- Answer questions and clear up misconceptions but do not try to give children all the information available about a news story. The best guide is to follow the child's lead, giving small pieces of information at a time and seeing how the child responds, before deciding what to say next.

- Look for opportunities to help children learn alternatives to the violence they hear about on the news. One effective way to do this is to point to examples from the children's own experience. For instance, you might say, "I get really upset when people solve their problems by hurting each other. Remember when you got really angry at Sandy for____? You didn't hurt her. You told her____." It is also important to make positive conflict resolution a regular part of your curriculum.[38]

- Recognize and support young children's efforts to work out what they have heard through their play, drawing, and other activities. This, regardless of anything else you do, can serve a very therapeutic role for children.

- Keep parents informed about your efforts to work with their children on troubling news events. Help parents figure out ways to limit the amount of real-world violence that their children see in the media.

ACTION IDEA

Use the chart above to help facilitate discussions with other adults on these issues.

Helping Children Take Action

One morning Jonah marched into his kindergarten classroom and held up an action figure (based on a popular TV program and movie) that was missing a leg. He indignantly told his friends that the toy had been his favorite birthday present, but that the second time he played with it, the leg fell off. He didn't think it was fair!

The other children jumped in to describe their own experiences with toys that had broken. The teacher saw that the children had intense feelings about their broken toys. She suggested they bring in their broken toys to talk about them at a class meeting the next day.

At the meeting the children talked at length about the toys—how and why each had broken, how they felt when it broke, their sense of unfairness about it breaking, and how the toy could have been made so that it wouldn't break.

Then the teacher asked for ideas about what the children could do about their broken toys. The children enthusiastically came up with some interesting suggestions:

"Have a funeral and bury them."

"Don't get any more toys like those that broke."

"Be gentle and don't fight with toys."

"Make a toy hospital where the toys can go to get fixed."

"Take the broken toys to the toy store where they came from, so the owner of the store knows which toys break too easily."

"Write a letter to the toy factories to say they shouldn't make toys that look so good but break so easy."

The teacher helped the children choose two action approaches. They made a toy hospital (where the children tried to fix their toys) and wrote letters to the toy manufacturers.

For children to become responsible and contributing members of society, they must learn how to participate actively in that society. They also need to believe that what they do can really make a difference. Children learn these lessons best when they have many opportunities to take action and see the concrete impact their actions have on their immediate environment. As they do this, the foundations are laid for knowing appropriate ways to take action on things they really care about and for developing a voice to be heard in their wider community.

The scenario above illustrates the kind of process that helps children build the foundation they need to become active participants in society. It is a process by which children learn to identify and understand problems they really care about and want to change, formulate possible solutions to the problems, and develop a repertoire of action ideas and skills they can use to work toward those solutions.

Media can undermine children's ability to participate

There are several ways that media, media violence, and media-linked toys make it hard for children to develop the attitudes and skills they need to feel empowered to take action:

Secondhand experience. When children watch TV, they interact indirectly with their world; in this secondhand experience, they passively observe others doing things and reacting to situations. What children really need to become problem solvers and active participants in their world is a lot of firsthand experience.

Imitative play. Media-linked toys often channel children into imitating what they see in the media rather than actively developing their own scripts based on their own needs. Imitative play can reduce children's opportunities to experience the kind of power that comes from trying out and seeing how their own ideas and actions can affect their world.

Violence as the way to feel powerful. Children see again and again in media and through media-linked toys that violence provides an acceptable, even desirable, way to solve problems and wield power. Instead of experiencing the *real,* lasting power that can come from having a meaningful impact on their environment and the people in it, children experience only the fleeting *pseudo*-power that comes from imitating media violence.

Dependence on the media. As children's ability to feel powerful and effective is undermined, their ability to resist the pull of media and media violence also is weakened. A vicious cycle can be set up whereby children "need" media, media violence, and media-related toys to feel strong. But what they really need are opportunities to feel strong through their own positive actions.

Empowering children to take action that grows out of their own needs

It is important to remember that, because of how children learn, teaching them how to take responsible action is a slow process, built gradually over time—with age and experience. The goal is not to show children a "one right way" to think about and respond to a problem or to further the agenda of adults; rather it is to teach them how to come up with strategies that make sense to them.

The more that efforts to help children take action are connected to their experiences, interests, and level of development, the more they will learn. This means working on problems directly connected to children's immediate experience and environment—the people, objects, behaviors, and routines in their daily lives. And it means helping them take actions where they can directly try out their ideas and experience the effects.

The kind of process to aim for occurs in the classroom scenario about broken toys at the beginning of this chapter. The children have an opportunity to say what they think, work out their own ideas, hear what others think, come up with their own action plan, and then try out the plan to see how it works. The adult, of course, has a vital role to play in helping the children successfully think through the action-taking process and translate their ideas into actions.

WHAT YOU CAN DO

Help children take action on matters that they really care about in their own lives.

In the current media culture, many children need special adult help in learning how to take actions that result in the effects they desire. It is often the children who get into the most trouble—those who show aggressiveness or lack impulse control—who need the most help. When they think they have few other avenues, children may resort to violence to get their needs met. Widening children's opportunities to take responsible action helps them become responsible members of the classroom community and beyond. It also helps them become willing and able to take action around media and media violence issues. As you help children take action, remember that the process they go through in coming up with a plan is often as important to their learning as what plan they come up with.

In a typical classroom day, take note of the opportunities children have to take responsible action and how they go about doing it. Pay attention to such issues as which children do and do not seem comfortable with the action-taking process and the times when children can take a greater role in decisionmaking and in devising action strategies.

___

Give children many opportunities to solve problems and take responsible actions on media and media culture issues in their own lives.

There are many ways to use this kind of media problem-solving and action-taking process to help children see how their actions can have a meaningful effect in their own lives. With parents and siblings at home, children can raise media issues that they work on in school. For example, children's letters to parents about TV rules, in Chapter 5, opened up family discussions and led to negotiation of what and how much TV to watch.

Children also can play an active role in influencing family decisions about how to deal with media-linked toys. Teachers can help children translate class discussions about "good" and "bad" toys into guidelines for parents about choosing toys. One teacher began this process by discussing the gifts that children give to others—for instance, birthday gifts to friends. The children talked about their ideas of "good" and "bad" toys and their understanding of consumerism, as well as how to take the perspective of the person who would receive the gift (not an easy task for young children). In leading the discussion, here are some of the key questions the teacher asked:

• How do you decide what to give for a gift?

• What makes a good gift?

• How can you know if someone will like a particular gift?

• How much money do you need to spend for it to be a good gift? What gifts can you give that don't cost any money?

• What kinds of things can you make as a gift? (The Shoe Box Kit Ideas in Chapter 6 might help children get started here.)

• Are there things you can *do* for others as a gift?

• If you decide on a toy for a gift, how do you know if it is a "good" toy? (The Toy Selection Guide in Chapter 6 can help with this discussion.)

When having the discussion about "good" and "bad" gifts, make a list of the children's ideas. Send it home so families will be aware of alternatives when making gift-giving decisions.

Help children become activists, using what they learn about media and media culture to educate others and promote change.

Children can take action within their own school settings and beyond to teach other children and adults about the media. Bulletin board displays, child-made posters, and presentations in other classrooms and at larger school meetings provide opportunities for children to realize that they can make a difference.

ACTION IDEA

Children can write letters and brochures which they read or send to other children about what they have learned about media and media culture. The letter from Youth Enlightening Youth in Chapter 4 is one example of children doing this.

In one school, as part of a study of toy advertising and the media, the fifth and sixth graders designed a brochure for younger children. Small groups of the older children went from class to class to read the brochure to the younger children and to lead discussions.

Here is an example of a guide prepared by fifth and sixth graders for the younger children in their school. It grew out of a unit of study on advertising on TV. In small groups, the older children went to younger children's classrooms to distribute and discuss the guide.

Children's Guide to TV Advertising

This is a brochure created by Sarah & Patty's 5 & 6 class, as part of our Media Project. It is a guide for younger kids to tell them what to look for in advertisements. During the Media Project, we watched a lot of advertisements and had class discussions about them; we also came up with a lot of ideas on what we watched. This brochure is a result of what we did for our Media Project.

• You don't have to buy "girl toys," like Barbie dolls, if you are a girl and "boy toys," like action figures, if you are a boy. There is no such thing as "girls' toys" or "boys' toys" because you can buy any toy you want. Girls don't have to like pink just because there is pink in the ads, and if you are a boy you don't have to like dark colors if boys like dark colors in the ads.

• Ads don't represent real kids. In the commercials, boys only play with "boy toys" and girls with "girl toys," but that's not true in real life because you can play with any toy you want. Even though there are a lot of white kids who play with toys in the commercials, that doesn't mean that only white kids play with toys in real life. Different kids of color like Black kids, Asian kids, and Native American kids all play with toys.

• Listen to what the announcer (person who is talking) says at the end of the commercial. Usually the most important things are said at the end and they are said really fast so that you won't hear that you will have to spend more money on accessories and batteries.

• Pay attention to what the toy really does. For example, sometimes in the commercials the toy moves by itself, but in real life it does not.

• Find out how much a toy costs before you decide you want it. Commercials usually don't tell you how much toys cost.

Children also can learn to express their views and take action in the wider community and with the media and toy industry. For example, children can write letters to broadcasters, toy manufacturers, toy stores, and government officials about the ideas generated in the classroom. (The addresses of major toy manufacturers, TV stations, and public officials are in the Resources section at the end of this book.) Here's a multipurpose letter that one class developed:

Dear [company name]:

Our _____ grade class at the _____ school is learning about media violence. We are writing to you to talk about [show/video/toy]. We think it is [good/bad] for children because_____

_____

_____

_____

_____

_____.

We hope you will listen to kids and [keep having shows like this one/replace this violent show that is unhealthy for children/make toys that help children play without violence].

Sincerely,

Using a format like the one provided above, here are examples of two letters children wrote to voice their opinions—positive and negative—about children's TV programs.

---

your street
your town & state
date

Dear Sir or Madame,

My name is _____Brenden_____. I am in second grade at Marstons Mills Elementary School. In my class we have been learning about kids and media.

I am writing to you to talk about the show _X-MeN_ _____ that airs on your network. I don't think the show is good for kids because _Fighting_ _woNPen's. litter kids cope the Move's_ _Like a PuNcha and kids._ _____.

I hope you will listen to kids and put on shows that are healthy for kids and fun to watch!

Sincerely,
Brenden (your name)

---

your street _tanrBarck_
your town & state _M 9_
date _13G_

Dear Sir or Madame,

My name is _Kyle_. I am in second grade at Marstons Mills Elementary School. In my class we have been learning about kids and media.

I am writing to you to talk about the show _Wishbone_ _____ that airs on your network. I think the show is great because _it is a non-racist_ _Show. Mixture of books and_ _Real life._
You should put 10 hours of wishbone every day
I hope you continue to put on great shows for kids!

Sincerely,
Kyle (your name)

Encourage children to work on class letters together. This works especially well with younger children who cannot write and also with issues that several children care about. Make sure children have opportunities to comment on what they think is good as well as on what concerns them. Also help them write about what they think should happen to make things better.

Guidelines for Helping Children Learn to Take Action

- Make sure children know that, even though they can contribute, it is the job of adults to make the world a safe place for children. Children should not think that their safety and well-being are dependent on their own actions.

- As children plan what actions to take, do not expect them to plan the same effective actions an adult may take. They cannot fully think through the logic of their ideas. As long as safety is assured, children need to try out ideas to see how they work.

- Choose topics for action in which children are likely to experience some kind of direct effect of their actions. For instance, it is often more meaningful for children to do something around issues that directly affect their lives or will provide them with a direct response.

- Choose action areas in which you are comfortable sharing your power and control with the children. While your input is vital to any successful actions, the children will probably come up with action plans that differ from ones you would use if it were up to you.

- Make sure the children are working on their own issues and ideas rather than those on the agenda of adults.

WORKING OUTSIDE
THE CLASSROOM

Teachers and Parents Working Together

Most of children's exposure to media, media violence, and media culture occurs in the home. Therefore, connecting with parents is a vital part of enhancing our efforts with children. As we reach out to parents, it is important to match what we do to the realities and stresses of parenting in a society where violent media and popular culture make the job of parenting even harder than it otherwise would be.

The realities for parents

Most parents welcome meaningful input—both in learning more about the nature of the problem of media violence and how it affects children and in developing strategies for dealing with it. But the job of dealing effectively with media violence in the home is a difficult one. Few parents—even those who seem the most conscientious and have the most resources—are fully satisfied with the results of their efforts, and many report frustration. They say they

• would like to find more support for their efforts.

• are frustrated at the experts who tell them to "just say no" to media violence and media-linked violent toys yet do not seem to have a clue about the realities of dealing with these issues in daily life.

• feel guilty and embarrassed at their failure to adequately deal with the problem.

• resent the blame that is often unfairly put on them for not being able to protect their children from the harmful aspects of media and media culture.

In the next chapter, the chart titled "12 Reasons Why 'Just Saying No' to Violent Media and Popular Culture Isn't Enough" explains some of the difficulties and complexities parents face in trying to deal adequately with media and media violence in the home. It illustrates why it is so important to get beyond putting the entire burden on parents and why teachers should avoid falling into the blame-the-parents trap, which serves only to separate teachers from parents and thwarts efforts to deal effectively with the media and media violence in children's lives.

ACTION IDEA

Copy the chart in Chapter 10 (12 Reasons Why "Just Saying No" to Violent Media and Popular Culture Isn't Enough). Use it to encourage parents and other colleagues to work with you to develop strategies for dealing with media violence. Also use it to present arguments in the wider community about why putting the entire burden of dealing with media violence on parents is wrong-headed and unfair.

Strength in mutual respect and collaboration

Finding an approach that fits the diversity of your children and parents is not always easy. Parents have a wide range of perspectives on media issues. They also differ considerably in their interest, ability, and resources. As you begin to work together, it is important to provide opportunities for voicing different points of view and, to the fullest extent possible, for finding common ground. The give-and-take discussion and win-win problem-solving techniques for working on media issues with children described throughout this book can be used effectively with parents. The teacher who raised her concerns at a parent conference about Tommy's exposure to news violence took just such an approach (see Chapter 7).

Despite your best efforts, some parents will be more open than others. Had Tommy's parents responded to the teacher's question by saying, "We need to have the TV on when we get home so we can make dinner," the teacher could have helped them come up with other things Tommy could do as they prepared dinner instead of watching the news. And if they had said something like, "We haven't seen the TV news create any problems for him," the teacher might have responded, "Well, I'm glad to hear that, because based on what he's said here, I wasn't sure." She could have continued to watch and work with Tommy on these issues at school but respected the parents' view—unless, of course, her concerns increased and she had to raise the issue again. But her initial conversation with the parents might still have led them to pay closer attention to how news reports affected Tommy.

The more you succeed at creating an ongoing process between teachers and parents and among parents themselves, the easier it is for everyone to deal with media issues. When children see adults working together on issues and sharing approaches and practices, they become more accepting of their own parents' efforts to deal with media issues. And parents feel more in control of the kinds of media their children are involved with, even during visits to other homes.

WHAT YOU CAN DO

Work to involve parents in efforts to address media and media violence issues.

In addition to the concrete ideas and examples for working with parents suggested in this and the next chapter, many of the other activities in this book can be adapted for your efforts to create home-school connections.

Share your concerns with parents about the problems created for children by violence and other inappropriate aspects of the media and media culture.

Because violence is often the aspect of the media that parents feel most negatively about, it can be an effective place to begin your efforts. Use or adapt the following letter about the problem of media violence and what parents can do to enlist parents' support for and involvement in your efforts. Survey parents to gauge what kind of specific information, guidance, and support they would like.

ACTION IDEA

Use the letter on pages 122–23 either for parents in your own class or for broader school-based efforts.

A Letter to Parents about Media Violence and Children

Dear Parents:

[I am/We are] concerned about how media violence and toys marketed with violent TV shows are teaching violence to children. [I/We] hope you will read this letter to learn more about why [I'm/we're] concerned and how we can begin to work together on this vital issue.

Facts about media violence in children's lives

- By the end of elementary school, the average child will have seen 8,000 murders and 100,000 other violent acts in the media.

- Children's cartoons and action programs average more than 20 acts of violence per hour, compared with 5 acts per hour during prime-time hours.

- The sale of Mighty Morphin Power Ranger products (based on the extremely violent children's TV show) surpassed $1 billion in 1994.

- More than $3 billion of products related to the *Star Wars* movie have been sold worldwide.

- In one survey, more than 90% of teachers thought the Power Rangers led to increased violence among the children they taught.

Media violence teaches children that

- fighting is the acceptable way to solve conflicts;

- violence is a common, normal part of everyday life;

- violence is fun and exciting; and

- the world is a dangerous place, so fighting is necessary.

Let's work together to reduce the harm media violence is doing to our children

For too long, parents have been told it's their job alone to deal with the problems created for their children by media violence. [I/We] think this places an unfair burden on parents. Media violence is creating problems too serious and complex in homes, schools, and the wider society for any one group to be able to solve on its own.

Many groups, including coalitions of physicians, educators, and parents, have begun to work together to create a community-wide effort to deal with this serious public health issue. As part of that effort, [I/we] will be working with the children in [my classroom/our school].

[I/We] will keep you posted about what we do and how you can help. [I/We] welcome your ideas and input. The more closely we can work together, the more we will be able to help your child resist the problems created by violence in the media. In the meantime, here are a few ideas to help you begin to think about what you can do.

How families can work on media violence issues

- Keep TV sets out of children's bedrooms and in a more public place.

- Work out limits on the amount of TV viewing.

- Try to plan in advance what programs will be watched.

- Try to select programs designed to promote children's positive development and learning (for instance, those on public television).

- Limit viewing of violent (and other noneducational) programming as much as possible.

- Watch TV together as a family when you can.

- Talk about what your child sees on TV—including such topics as what is real and what is not, distinguishing between ads and shows, solving conflicts without using violence, what you and your child liked and did not like about a show.

- Try not to buy products directly linked to violent TV shows or that are advertised heavily during violent programs.

- Choose toys that promote creativity, can be played with in many ways, and will stay interesting over a period of time.

- Work outside the home to reduce the levels of violence in children's media. Involve others too, including your children, other family members, and other parents.

- Call local TV stations to express your opinions. Make a list of phone numbers to keep by the phone.

- Ask us, your child's teachers and school, for help and support.

Thank you for working with [me/us].

[Your name and/or your school's name]

When specific issues or concerns about media come up in your classroom, use them as opportunities to work with and educate parents.

The following letter, from a child care center director to parents, focuses on superheroes that the teachers believed contribute to violence in their classrooms. Giving parents concrete examples from daily classroom life about how media violence directly affects their children can be a very effective way to elicit parents' understanding and support.

Heroes vs. Superheroes

Dear Parents:

The problem

We have been having trouble at school with Batman, Ninja Turtles, Power Rangers [add or substitute the superheroes you are confronted with], and other violent media superheroes. Throughout my years of experience as a parent and teacher, children have engaged in pretend play about superheroes. Parents and teachers, in the past, have worked to monitor and place limits on that type of play, but a certain amount of superhero play did not seem to adversely affect young children.

The recent crop of superheroes, however, are of a different type, and children are getting hurt and scared. The number and frequency of excessively violent acts, the opportunity to view these repeatedly on videotape, and the relentless marketing of associated products have created a world in which children are bombarded with superhero hype. Is it any wonder children are so obsessed with these characters?

Many parents I work with would *like* to keep their children away from the influence of today's superheroes but do not want them to feel isolated from the peer social group. The pressure of the group is to acquire as many Power Ranger, Ninja Turtle, Batman, etc., toys, videos, clothing items, and accessories as possible. These are what children want for gifts, and they have become status items. Every teacher I talk with feels that the violent language and actions that accompany this type of play reduce a child's capacity to pretend anything else and interfere with his or her ability to solve conflicts thoughtfully and nonaggressively.

Some solutions

It is clear that a partnership effort between home and school is required to solve this problem. Together we must determine what is in the best interests of the children we love and care for. At this time [your center] is recommending a course of action that requires your feedback.

1. **We need to de-emphasize superheroes and cut down on our children's exposure to them,** as well as to much adult-oriented media material. Many children are aggressive enough under normal circumstances, even without superheroes to imitate. Since young children are learning to distinguish reality from fantasy, they do not understand that what they see is pretend or a cartoon. They are not sophisticated enough to deal with the powerful imagery portrayed. Sleep problems, agitated behavior, withdrawal, and aggression are all ways in which children react to things that frighten them or threaten their safety.

2. **When we shop for new clothing, toys, or accessories, we can help our children select designs that do not convey a violent theme.** You may wish to say that [the center] or their teachers do not want these things at school because some children get scared. Help your child choose more creative toys and accessories.

3. **We can acknowledge that these characters are fun and exciting but that they also hurt other people—and fighting is not acceptable.** Young children are learning how to get along with others. They are learning how to express their feelings and desires with words rather than by hitting and pushing. These characters demonstrate that violence solves problems and that victims are not really hurt.

4. **We can help children learn to see both sides of an argument and settle differences with words.** This is most effective when we model this behavior ourselves within the family and the classroom. When parents shout at one another, when they are unable to resolve their differences, their children will also use this approach to solving problems. We need to exhibit those traits we most value and wish our children to acquire.

(continued on next page)

5. We can help children understand the true meaning of hero—that real heroes are people who work hard to make the world a better place through peaceful means. Parents are heroes; teachers are heroes; doctors, firefighters, and religious leaders are heroes. A power sword or gun doesn't make a person a hero! Rather, a hero has a sense of connection to and a responsibility for others in need, high standards of right and wrong, a commitment to friends and family, and the ability to see the other person's point of view. We can teach our children to be heroes!

You may recall the questionnaire that many of you completed last spring concerning your feelings about violence and how it affects your family. The results of that survey indicated your wish for the center to increase your awareness of the effects of this problem on children and to recommend what you might emphasize with your children at home. This letter is in response to that request. There will be a follow-up discussion on this subject during November. Watch for the date and time!

Halloween

While teachers really like to see children have fun with dress-ups, every year on Halloween we all dread the impact of superhero outfits worn by the children. A morning of children waving pretend weapons at one another and being ready to fight creates havoc, annoys and frightens children who do not like that kind of play, and serves no productive purpose.

We are asking, therefore, that superhero outfits not be worn to [your center] on Halloween Dress-Up Day. If you have already purchased or made your child's costume and it is a superhero outfit, please save it for trick-or-treating and help your child select another outfit for school (one without weapons, please). Some suggestions include community helper heros, storybook characters, animals, or fruits and vegetables. See your child's teachers for additional themes the children have enjoyed.

Teachers in the preschool classes will be discussing this request directly with the children so they know how their teachers feel about superheroes at school. Teachers also are planning to incorporate costumes worn by the children into a series of plays to be given that day for other classes.

Your cooperation in this matter is greatly appreciated.

When you hear of upcoming new movies or TV programs that may be of particular concern, take preventive measures by sending home "media alerts" that describe the nature of the problem and offer suggestions about what to do.

Send home other materials from this book that will help parents learn more about the problems created for children by media violence and media culture and that will give them strategies for responding.

Base your choice of items to send home on such things as specific issues you are working on with the children, issues you think your group of parents will be most receptive to, issues relevant for specific events (such as birthday parties or the release of a new violent children's movie), or particular times of years (such as the holiday gift-giving season).

Before the holiday gift-giving season, send home the Toy Selection Guide in Chapter 6. It can help parents make more informed and thoughtful toy choices.

Help parents learn more about choosing quality media programming for their children.

Throughout this book the focus primarily is on how to work to minimize the harmful effects media can have on children. But media are and will continue to be a part of children's lives, and there is a lot that adults can do to use media in positive ways—for instance, choose programming that matches children's developmental levels and needs.

At the same time, as the amount of programming proliferates, it becomes harder and harder for parents to keep track of and know what the best (and worst) programs, movies, and other forms of media are. Some parents lack access to information that can help them make informed choices about what their children watch. Much of the information that is most readily available comes from the media industry—for instance, from advertising, movie and video ratings, and the new ratings system designed for use with the V-chip (see Chapter 1).

Teachers have an important role to play in giving parents both a basic understanding of appropriate media for making informed decisions and access to resources that provide the information they need to choose appropriate media.

ACTION IDEA

Use the chart, A Developmental Framework for Assessing Children's Television, in Chapter 2, as a starting point for helping parents learn more about how to judge appropriate media for their children.

Provide parents with information about positive uses of media with their children.

Media, when used thoughtfully and appropriately, can offer positive avenues to children. As technology plays a greater and greater role in modern life, parents will need to know more and more about not only how to screen out the negative media but also how to help their children use media in positive ways.

One of the best ways to help parents with this is to learn about media and keep up-to-date on quality programming. Not only will this provide the information you need to make informed choices about how you work with children and use media in your classroom, but it also will give you the foundation you need to work with parents on these issues.

ACTION IDEA

Gather a few key resources on media programming that can assist parents in making positive media choices for their children. Put the materials in a location where parents can easily come and use them. Several such resources are listed in the Resources section at the end of this book.

Keep parents informed about what you are doing about media and media violence in the classroom and offer suggestions about how they can support these efforts at home.

If you have a regular newsletter for parents, use it to describe what you are doing in the classroom to help children deal with media and media violence, why you are doing it, and how parents can connect it to what they do at home. You may want to write a regular column or feature. Even if you do not have a regular newsletter, you could prepare a special issue describing your media activities.

ACTION IDEA

Try to involve the children in preparing a media newsletter. Young children can dictate information on and draw pictures about what they would like their parents to know. Older children can do the actual "reporting" about what they have learned and what they plan to do about what they have learned.

To build onto the curriculum you are doing with children, create media projects to send home that families can work on together. Some schools, in trying to make homework relevant and meaningful to children, call such projects *family homework*. In addition to providing simple directions, family homework often briefly explains to parents the reason for the activity and the issues to focus on.

Examples of activities that children and parents can do together on media issues include

• collecting data on child or family TV-viewing habits;

• writing a story about what families like to do together when they are not watching TV; or

• describing a TV advertisement that misled them or a media-linked toy that broke.

Family homework can help families begin to work on media violence issues together, as well as provide you with information for the class curriculum on media and media violence. Many of the activities in this book can be adapted for family homework projects.

Here is one example of a family homework activity. It involves graphing the TV a child watches for one week. The teacher sent home an enlarged photocopy of the graph as well as a letter to parents that explained the activity. (Fewer, bigger boxes work best with younger children).

Family Homework Activity: TV-Viewing Graph

Dear Parents:

Today in your child's class we began our media literacy work. We discussed what we like and dislike about TV, how much TV we watch, and family rules about television.

Accompanying this letter is a TV-Viewing Graph. This graph is designed as a "family homework" activity. Each night for a week, please help your child fill out the graph before he/she goes to bed. The graph will chart how much TV your child watched each day. For example, if your child watched three hours of television on Sunday, help him/her color in (with marker, crayon, or pencil) six half-hour blocks. Whenever possible, also record the names of the TV show in the appropriate block. Videos (movies) should be included in TV-viewing time.

The purpose of this graph is to explore how much TV we watch individually and as a class. We will examine our results next week, so please help your child remember to bring the completed graph back to school one week from today. Later on we will look at other things children do with their free time besides watch TV.

Please keep in mind that my intent is not to criticize or judge family TV-viewing habits and that there is no "right" or "wrong" answer in this activity.

I hope your family has fun doing this family homework together!

Sincerely,

TV-VIEWING GRAPH FOR _____

	Sunday	Monday	Tuesday	Wednesday	Thursday	Friday	Saturday
1/2 hour							
1/2 hour							
1/2 hour							
1/2 hour							
1/2 hour							
1/2 hour							
1/2 hour							
1/2 hour							
1/2 hour							

Please help your child fill in one box for each half hour of TV he or she watched. The child can color in the box and write the name of the show(s) and/or draw a little picture of the show in the box.

Support parents in their efforts to protect their children from the harmful effects of media violence and media-related violent toys and play.

Create a supportive classroom/school community in which parents and teachers help each other develop effective strategies for dealing with media violence and other hazards of media culture. Do things that help parents feel that they no longer must deal with these issues completely on their own. For example, schedule give-and-take discussions with parents about such issues as how they deal with media and media-related violence with their children, what their problems and concerns are (as well as what yours are), and how you can work together to deal with shared concerns. Remember, your efforts in the classroom can provide powerful starting points for building effective approaches for children and parents in their homes.

ACTION IDEA

Organize opportunities for parents to get together to

- discuss their successes, concerns, and struggles in dealing with media violence with their children; and

- work out common approaches to media violence and toys—for instance, how much and what TV shows children watch and video games they play, guidelines for toys, and which TV-linked toys and gifts are and are not okay for children to give each other.

Get parents involved in working outside their homes to reduce the quality and quantity of violence in media and popular culture.

Work with parents to organize school-wide and community-wide events that support change, such as toy gun trade-ins; TV program, movie, or toy boycotts; and TV turn-offs. Chapter 11 provides helpful information to get you started with such events.

ACTION IDEA

Help parents voice their opinions and concerns to TV and toy producers by copying and sending home the sample letters in Chapter 11. You also could include the list of addresses of where to write, which can be found in the Resources section.

Parents and Children
Working Together

A Special Note to Parents and Teachers about
Ways to Use This Chapter

This chapter is directed especially to parents—to help you develop approaches for dealing with media violence that can work for you and your children. Many of the underlying assumptions, goals, and approaches outlined for teachers in this book also can be put into practice in the home. And many of the ideas and materials connect with and supplement what is presented in this chapter. The media literacy resources listed in the Resources section will provide you with further assistance.

Teachers using this book may want to share this chapter directly with parents. Parents using this book on their own will find that this chapter helps make connections between the content and suggestions throughout the book and their experiences at home. In turn, some families also may want to share the book with their child's teachers and school.

Media and media violence intrude upon family life, often in unexpected ways. Here are four of the many experiences that parents have had with media encroachment upon their children's lives. These accounts poignantly illustrate the extent of the task before us all, in dealing with the whole range of potential ways that media culture can have a negative impact on children.

> I took my 5-year-old daughter to the hospital for an x-ray. In the waiting room, a soap opera was on the TV monitor. An angry man held a knife to the throat a terrified-looking woman and began to tear at her clothes to rape her. My daughter's eyes were glued to the screen. We went into the hall to wait. There were no controls to turn the TV off.

My son wanted to be a Power Ranger for the Halloween party in his kindergarten class. I put a lot of energy into getting him excited about being The Cat in the Hat, wearing a costume that we had fun inventing together. On Halloween he came home from school distraught and angry (mostly at me) because every other boy in his class was a Power Ranger and it "wasn't fair" he wasn't one. I felt bad for him. I'm sure next year it will be harder figuring out together what to do.

My son goes to a friend's house, where they spend whole days playing violent video games while the parents work (at home). I notice that after these days, Jules comes home really grumpy and often has a hard time sleeping. I tried talking to the friend's parents about the problem. They nicely told me they don't think their son has a problem playing video games while they work; if Jules has a problem, then he just shouldn't go to their house. I'm torn between the friendship (the boys are best friends) and my desire to limit Jules's video-game time and his exposure to video-game violence.

My wife and I work very hard to protect our 6-year-old daughter from violence in the media. Then she won a poster contest for a children's TV program sponsored by a local TV station. We excitedly went to get the prize. It turned out to be a six-video set of Power Ranger episodes.

Parents are often told that media and media violence are their problems. According to this notion, if parents just knew how to set limits with their children and would say no to media violence and toys, there would not be a problem with violence in media and popular culture.

Keeping the blame on parents is a convenient way to avoid dealing with the problem at a society-wide level. It also keeps the blame off those who benefit most from media violence: those who produce and market it. It is unrealistic and unfair that so much of the burden of dealing with media violence is put on parents' shoulders. Parents should be supported in their efforts to raise healthy and responsible children—and blaming only makes their job harder.

Even when families try to deal effectively with media and media violence in the home, they rarely solve the problem adequately. The media culture and its violent content permeate their children's lives, as evident in the examples above. Media are everywhere—from TV programs and movies to computers and video games, from media-linked toys in toy stores to media-linked food products at supermarkets, from TV monitors at airports and shopping malls to the "information superhighway" on the Internet.

The following chart maps out the reasons why "just saying no," as with most simplistic solutions to complex problems, is *not* an adequate option for dealing with the problem.

12 Reasons Why "Just Saying No" to Violent Media and Popular Culture Isn't Enough

1. **Just saying no doesn't solve the problem; children are exposed anyway.**

   - The media and toy industries know how to bypass parents and get directly to children.

   - The childhood culture is saturated with things parents are trying to say no to.

2. **By saying no, parents cut themselves off from what their kids are seeing, doing, and learning about violence in media and popular culture.**

   - Parents give up their role in helping to counteract the negative effects of media on their children.

3. **If something is in the environment, children need some way to try to figure it out, to make sense of it.**

   - Just saying no doesn't help children work through what they are exposed to in the popular culture.

4. **Just saying no doesn't help children learn to cope with what surrounds them and to be as healthy as possible in spite of it.**

   - It doesn't help children learn to be responsible people who can make responsible choices within the all-pervasive popular culture.

   - It also cuts them off from an important part of growing up in a media culture—actively finding ways to utilize media's positive aspects to enhance their development and learning.

5. **Parents can't say no to everything.**

   - There are too many things to say no to, so parents often say no only to the very worst things, letting in less offensive things that they still do not like.

   - Gradually, as parents say yes to the less disturbing things, the quantity and quality of the harmful items escalate.

6. **Saying no is exhausting.**

   - There's always more to say no to.

   - Because children don't passively accept our no's all of the time, enforcing the ban takes time and energy.

7. **Parents and children become alienated from each other at earlier and earlier ages.**

   - Power struggles are set up at early ages.

   - Children sneak to use the stuff when it's available.

   - They can feel guilty when they become involved in activities their parents disapprove of.

   - Children can be forced to make choices between their parents and their friends.

   - Over time the struggle undermines children's belief in the credibility and goodness of their parents and other adults.

8. **Children can feel isolated from their peers if their childhood culture is dominated by popular culture themes and they are forbidden to participate.**

9. **To "just say no" is too simplistic a response to a very complex issue that requires complex solutions.**

10. **Saying no is a complex process; there are many ways to say it.**

    - Saying no is a dynamic, not static, process.

    - Knowing how to say no in developmentally appropriate ways that take into account the complexities takes much thought, skill, time, and energy.

    - Done in a simple black-and-white way, saying no goes against conflict-resolution theory by providing adults win–children lose solutions to problems rather than allowing win-win solutions in which everyone's needs can be taken into account.

11. **Telling parents to say no puts unfair blame and burden on them.**

    - Parents end up feeling guilty and inadequate when they're told (by teachers, the government, and media and toy industries) that it's their job to say no to the popular culture—and they can't possibly fully succeed.

12. **Telling parents to say no can be very divisive; it undermines broad-based efforts to solve the problems created for children and society by violence in the media.**

    - Instead of parents, professionals, and policymakers working together to change the popular culture and stop the exploitation of children for profit, a wedge is driven between them, diverting and diluting their potential power to bring about positive change.

    - Race and class issues arise when many parents, whose coping skills are already stretched to the limits, are told by professionals to dictate prescribed responses.

It is important to find solutions that go beyond just saying no. Admonitions to "Limit your child's TV viewing," or "Don't use TV as a babysitter," or "Don't buy violent TV-linked toys" don't help either. Such simplistic rules

- fail to take into account the realities of parenthood today ("It's hard to monitor what my kids watch when I'm making dinner." "What am I supposed to do with my older children? They have a right to watch their shows too").

- do not adequately address the need to help children gradually learn to take responsibility and regulate their own relationships with the media.

- ignore the world outside the home, which, as we saw in the anecdotes at the beginning of this chapter, so often sabotages parents' efforts ("What about all the violent media-linked war toys my son's friends gave him for his birthday?").

Unfortunately, there are few simple rules for or solutions to the many problems families encounter with media culture and violence issues. At the same time there are endless ways that parents make an enormous difference in how the media culture affects their children. And parents can work on them in ways that enhance their relationship with their children.

The suggestions that follow are intended to show the kinds of things you can do to get started. Once you begin, you will need to forge your own solutions, ones tailored to your and your child's or children's unique situation. Choose those approaches that seem the most relevant and see where they lead. As you work with your children, please try to remember that a lot of what you do will be trial and error. Not all efforts will work, and you will rarely feel as if you are doing enough.

Important goals to aim for are to help your children resist the negative influences of media, media violence, and popular culture; learn to recognize and choose appropriate media; and become informed and responsible consumers of media. To accomplish these goals, children need to gradually develop the necessary attitudes, values, and skills—they cannot be handed them by decree. Then, as children get older, they will be prepared to gradually take on the responsibility themselves. The more you are able to make your efforts meaningful, respectful, and appropriate to the developmental levels of your children, the more impact you will have.

WHAT YOU CAN DO

Learn about the TV programs your child watches and wants to watch, as well as what is in the movies, videos, music, and other media in your child's life.

This will help you decide what is and is not okay for your child. It also will help you gather the information you need to talk with your child about the content of specific media and to work out viewing rules.

When possible, watch TV with your child and talk about what you see.

Use the following questions to help you get started. Keep in mind that the point is not to get "right" answers but to get used to talking about and sharing honest information with your child.

Questions to Help Parents and Children Talk about TV and Other Media

- Talk about your reactions—both positive and negative—to what you each see.

  "What did you think about that show/game?"

  "I liked it when _____ happened. What did you think about that?"

  "I didn't like it when _____ . I wish they didn't have to hurt each other. What do you think?"

- Help sort out fantasy from reality.

  "What was pretend and what was real? How could you tell?" (Help sort out points of confusion by saying things such as "In real life things don't work that way.")

  "I wonder how they made _____ happen on that show. What do you think?"

- Help children compare what they saw to their own experience.

  "Could anything like _____ happen in our lives? When? How would it be the same? different?"

  "What would you do if you were in that situation?"

- Talk directly about the violence and other mean-spirited behavior children see on the screen.

  "What do you think about how _____ solved her/his problem? If you had a problem like that, what could you do? or say?"

  "Can you think of a way to solve that problem so that no one gets hurt or everyone stays safe?"

- Ask questions that focus on stereotyped images and behaviors.

  " I wonder why it's always men with big muscles who go to fight. Did you notice that? What do you think about it?"

  "It seems like the women always need to get rescued by the men. Have you noticed that? I wonder why."

  "I wonder why the 'bad guys' have foreign accents. Or why they always wear dark colors."

Videotape appropriate shows that your child likes to watch. The taped programs can be used to have a good show on hand at times when it's okay for your child to watch but there is nothing good on, or you can view it together and talk about the show in a more thorough fashion—stopping, replaying, analyzing as you go.

Try to find out what programs your children watch when you are not with them—either in your own home or at other houses.

Use the questions on page 139 to talk to your children about what they saw, especially if they saw something you would not have wanted them to see.

Work with your children to make meaningful and age-appropriate routines and to negotiate rules for using media responsibly.

The more meaningful and understandable a rule is for a child, the more likely the rule will work. Children need to feel their voices are heard as adults lead them through a process of making media rules. Then they feel like responsible participants and understand the decisions reached.

Making rules with young children is an ongoing process; no solution will work forever. As children try out a rule and see how it works, as they get older, as media change, as family needs change—each of these factors necessitates renegotiation of the rules. Rather than seeing this amending process as an indication that rules don't work, it can be useful for parents to realize that this process is part of helping children gradually become responsible consumers of media, even when a vigilant adult is not present.

Five-year-old Joan's growing habit of watching TV has begun to worry her father. One evening Joel sits down beside Joan and initiates a give-and-take discussion.

Joel: I've noticed you're watching a lot of TV lately. Today, Joan, you woke up, watched *Sesame Street,* then *Mr. Rogers' Neighborhood,* and went to school. When you got home you watched *Batman* before dinner. Now you're watching *Carmen Sandiego.* It will be bedtime soon. You haven't played with one toy today. I haven't played with you, and I really miss that. It's just too much TV when there's so little time at home. We have to figure out something to do so we have time for all the things we like to do. What do you think we can do?

Joan: I have to see *Batman.* That's my favorite.

Joel: We've talked about *Batman.* I know you like that a lot, and we said that was okay. What I'm worried about now is how much time you're watching. That's the problem. Is there some way you can choose which shows to watch and still have time left over for family time and play? Like maybe, if you see *Batman,* we could make the rule, No watching TV after dinner.

Joan: But I just started watching *Carmen Sandiego,* and I like that too—oh I know! I'll take turns!

Joel: How would that work? You mean one night you'll watch *Batman* and the next night watch *Carmen Sandiego*? [Joan nods in agreement.] That sounds like it might solve the problem. Let's try it and see how it works.

ACTION IDEA

Have give-and-take discussions with your child, as Joel does in this dialogue, to work out rules and routines for media use in and out of the home.

Joan and Joel come up with a solution to their problem. It is a solution that takes into account both of their points of view. Joel fully assumes his vital roles as a media gatekeeper and educator. At the same time, he frames the discussion in terms that Joan can understand and see how to put the solution into practice. Such an approach will help her develop her own internal controls and a sense of commitment to making the solution work. As children get older and gain experience working out solutions, they are able to play a greater role in the problem-solving process and come up with more elaborate solutions.

In working out their solution, here is the process that Joan and Joel used:

> ## A Problem-solving Process for Parents and Children
>
> - Talk about the problem together in a way that helps your child see both sides of the issue without making critical value judgments.
>
> - Try to come up with one or more possible solutions. Talk about how each one might work in practice and whether it could work for both of you.
>
> - Choose a solution that you both agree on, one that takes into account each other's ideas, issues, and concerns.
>
> - Help your child try out the solution and see how it works by directly experiencing the consequences.
>
> - Later on, talk together about how the solution worked and decide whether and how it should be amended to make it work better.

ACTION IDEA

As you begin to use this problem-solving process to develop media rules and routines and to work out media-related issues with your child, start very simply. Provide concrete structure and information—for instance, "You can watch this show or that show after breakfast. Let's talk about which one to choose."

You can use this kind of problem-solving discussion process to determine

- what TV programs, videos, video games, etc., are and are not okay to watch.

- how much screen time is okay. *Screen time* equals the time spent in front of a screen—any screen (whether it be a TV show, movie on the VCR or in the theater, video game, or computer). Rather than a separate time limit for each kind of screen, the inclusive screen time provides an effective and meaningful organizer for dealing with the overall amount of time spent involved with media.

- when it is okay or not okay to watch TV and/or use other media. Planning *what* will be watched and *when* gives children the structure they need to get into a predictable and manageable media routine. They learn to avoid impulse viewing.

Problem-solving discussion can also help determine

- what to do when the TV and other media are turned off. Many children experience *PTVT* (post-TV trauma) when they turn off the TV or video game and have to figure out what to do next. Turning off the television (or any media activity) involves shifting from the fast-paced clip of a world that someone else has created to invention and reconnection to one's own resources. Many children have a hard time with this transition. Make the transition easier for them by offering a range of simple things they can do—set the table for dinner, ask you or another family member to read them a book, or draw a picture with conveniently located crayons and paper. The more you can help your children develop a range of appealing interests and activities to do, both with you and by themselves, the easier it will be for them to resist the pull of the nearest TV or computer.

- and what to do about media-linked toys and other media-linked products. Toys that are marketed with TV shows and other media, especially those that are violent, present special problems for children.[39] They can undermine play, creativity, and imagination as children imitate the violent plots they have seen on the screen; keep children focused on the violent content they see, thereby putting an unhealthy emphasis on fighting in their play; and lead to an exaggerated focus on consumerism—the desire to continually buy more and the belief that specific toys are necessary to have fun and play "right."

Plan toy and media-related product purchases in advance. Keep a list of the things your child asks for. Together, go over it periodically to determine which items seem like the "best" choices and why. Cross off items no longer wanted. Use the list when it is time to make a gift purchase.

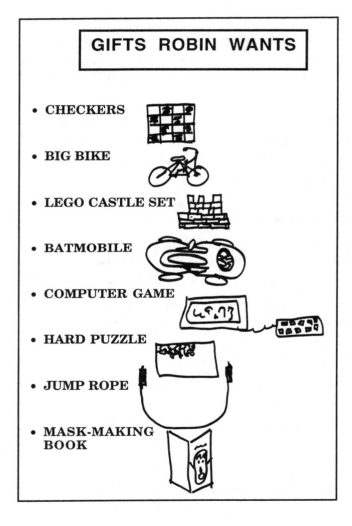

GIFTS ROBIN WANTS

- CHECKERS
- BIG BIKE
- LEGO CASTLE SET
- BATMOBILE
- COMPUTER GAME
- HARD PUZZLE
- JUMP ROPE
- MASK-MAKING BOOK

This list of "Gifts Robin Wants" was kept on the refrigerator with a magnet. With the help of his mom, 5-year-old Robin kept adding to it as new items came up. The illustrations helped him "read" the list so he could cross out things he got or no longer wanted. Older children can add on new items themselves and draw their own illustrations.

When 7-year-old Emil wanted a Nintendo video-game system for his birthday, his parents used the five-part give-and-take discussion process to debate the purchase. In this process the family negotiated the following list of rules and dealt with many of the issues discussed in this chapter: screen time, consumerism, violence, toys, and play. The list was posted in the kitchen on the refrigerator.

Emil's Rules for Nintendo

1. My video-game playing time counts as "screen time."

2. I can't get really violent games. Mostly I'll get games that aren't fighting.

3. I can play only one hour a day. If I play more, Nintendo gets put away for a week.

4. I can't play more than four hours a week. If I play more, Nintendo gets put away for a week.

5. I have to stop when you call me. If I don't stop in five minutes, Nintendo gets put away for a week.

6. I can get only three games a year—for my birthday, for Chanukah, and at one other time.

7. If I nag for a new game, Nintendo goes away for a week.

8. I can't play when a friend comes over (unless there's a new game).

9. If anyone thinks a rule isn't working well, we can talk about ways to change it.

Network with other parents and your child's teachers on efforts to deal with the hazards of media in children's lives.

Despite your best efforts to work with your children on media issues, they no doubt will be exposed to the media culture outside your home in ways that are hard for you to control. Developing a dialogue with the other adults in your child's life to about how to deal with media and which media is and is not okay is key to creating a less toxic media environment for children and to building a community of concerned adults who convey to children their shared media concerns and decisions. Working together helps everyone feel less isolated and more effective in their efforts. The previous chapter on parents and teachers working together and the following chapter on community building provide many examples of how others have worked together on these issues.

Work with other parents, teachers, and your community to promote the positive and reduce the negative aspects of media culture in the wider society.

While there is much that you can do in the home to reduce the harmful effects of media culture on your child, no amount of effort is a substitute for the creation of a more positive media culture for children in the overall society. The more we can work together to bring about more broad-based change, the easier all of our jobs with our own children will be. And the more we will contribute to the creation of a more positive environment for all children to grow up in. The chapter on building community that follows as well as the Resources section will help you with this sometimes over-whelming task. The more of us who find our own special ways to pitch in with efforts both big and small, the more of an impact we all can have.

11

Community Building for Change

Almost every industrialized country in the world—except the United States—sees creating an appropriate media environment for its children as a legitimate role of government. As world-renowned pediatrician T. Berry Brazelton clearly points out,

> TV is a very powerful medium. It's the biggest competitor for our children's minds and hearts, and we'd better pay attention to it . . . . I was put on a commission by the Clintons to try to regulate prime time [television] for children and we ran headlong into business. They said we were violating the First Amendment. They wouldn't let us touch it. And yet, every country in Europe, Australia, even China, has regulations on children's prime time. So we are the only country that puts business ahead of children and families. Parents had better get with it and figure out what they're going to do about it.[40]

When a society does not take seriously its responsibility to protect children from unhealthy media, the people who care about the well-being of children must take on the responsibility themselves.

This book has shown how teachers, parents, and children, working together, can play a vital role in combating the effects of media, media violence, and media culture on children's lives. But adults' and children's efforts in homes and classrooms provide only one piece of the solution. Also addressed must be the problem itself and its root causes: the current media culture is harming children and the wider society is not taking responsibility for creating a cultural environment that supports the healthy development of children.

Meaningful acts, by all of us, will contribute to the critical mass that is needed to promote positive change. Early childhood educators are trained to promote the learning, development, and well-being of young children, and they have the knowledge and skills that are needed to work in the wider community to create a healthier environment in which to raise children. And parents are in a position to have more impact on the role of media in their children's lives than anyone else. By joining forces, parents and teachers have a powerful voice for creating a healthier childhood media culture.

School communities are ideally suited to mobilize efforts, large and small, for change. What follows are ideas about the kinds of activities that can mobilize school communities to work together to create an environment for children that supports healthy development in the media culture; protects children from the harmful aspects of media, media violence, and the media culture; and seeks to change societal acceptance of media practices that market violence to children.

Try to tailor what you do to the needs, resources, and schedules of your particular families, school, and wider community so that many people and groups will find ways to participate and make meaningful contributions. Community actions like those that follow can help recreate the human connections and sense of empowerment that have been so seriously undermined by the isolation created by the media in our lives.

WHAT YOU CAN DO

Work to get your school community involved in efforts to combat the hazards of media culture in children's lives.

Encourage school administrators and others in the community to support and take an active role in your efforts. The more people you can get to work together and develop shared strategies for dealing with media issues, the greater will be the impact of your efforts on children's lives and in the wider community.

Plan presentations and initiate discussions at school-wide staff meetings, inservice training, and parent evenings. Such efforts help create a climate in which talking about and working on media issues is a normal part of life in the school community.

ACTION IDEA

Prepare a parent and/or teacher presentation on media and media violence issues. One of the educational videos listed in the Resources section would provide a lively starting point for discussion. Also use the materials in this book. In the discussion, try to come up with an action plan the group can begin to work on.

Establish a resource collection with information and resources that will help parents and others in the community learn more about media and children issues.

The organizations listed in the Resources section provide information about many inexpensive resources you can easily collect. In addition, a growing number of sites on the World Wide Web provide useful information and resources that can be down-loaded and printed. Encourage people to copy the educational materials/brochures and distribute them as widely as possible in your community.

The resource collection also can include materials that review and recommend appropriate media for children. For instance, include *The Kids First! Directory: A Consumer's Guide to Quality Children's Videos and CD-ROMs* (available from the Coalition for Quality Children's Media, which is listed in the Resources section).

ACTION IDEA

Set up an informational display table with media violence educational resources at community events. This can help you connect with other people and groups interested in working on media violence issues.

Help organize school-wide activities that help parents and children understand the effects of media and media violence in their lives and develop strategies for positive change.

In recent years several kinds of events have been designed to help school communities work together on media issues. Often they began as grassroots efforts and were so successful that schools in other communities decided to participate too.

You can organize a media turn-off event, for instance, a TV Turn-off Week, TV-Violence Turn-off Week, or a Screen-time Turn-off Weekend. These are becoming an increasingly common and effective approach for schools around the country to begin working on media efforts. There is even an officially designated, annual TV Turn-off Week. National and local organizations that promote school- and community-sponsored turn-off events are listed in the Resources section.

As you begin to work out the kind of turn-off you want to organize in your setting, here are a few issues to keep in mind:

- Think about what you hope children, families, schools and the wider community will learn from the turn-off experience. Rather than just seeing if participants can get through a week without TV or violent TV shows, or if they can avoid all screen time, the most meaningful and effective approach is to help families use the turn-off as an opportunity to reflect on the role of TV and other media in their lives.

- Help children and families prepare for what a week without TV or screen time will be like. Will it apply equally to all family members? At what times will it be hardest for which family members? When do various family members rely most on TV? What can they do instead? How can children and grown-ups deal with the potential problems and challenges that may come up when they have to find something to do instead of watching TV?

- Be prepared to help participants reflect on the experience as it is occurring and deal with unanticipated problems that come up.

- Help participants plan ahead for what will happen after the turn-off. For instance, during TV Turn-off Week at one school, volunteers played board games with children at lunch (the videotapes children usually saw at lunch recess were not allowed during the turn-off). The games were so popular that, after the week was over, the school arranged for the game volunteers to return once a week.

- Help children and families honestly buy into, not feel coerced into, participating.

Prepare materials, like the ones developed by the Winnetka Alliance for Early Childhood (see Appendix B), that will help turn the turn-off event into a learning experience for the whole family. For instance, you can develop a Turn-off Certificate to help families talk about and decide together whether to sign onto the community-wide media turn-off effort.

You also can plan other community events, like a used toy exchange, to promote the use of healthy toys. Toy exchanges help families shift the focus of toys away from the heavy emphasis on consumerism. They also provide more toy opportunities for families with limited financial means.

You can organize events, such as toy-gun trade-ins and community-wide educational campaigns about toys of violence, that reduce the proliferation of violent, media-linked toys. Such efforts can provide opportunities for parents and children to talk about violent toy issues in a supportive community context.

Try to get local toy stores involved. The following flyer accompanied one community's efforts to organize a toy-gun buy-back campaign in conjunction with local toy stores.

The Cambridge Campaign Against Toys of Violence

What is the campaign?

We are a group of Cambridge residents—parents, teachers, students, officials, and store owners—who are working with the Cambridge Peace Commission and the Peaceable Schools Center at Lesley College to sponsor activities that protest the marketing of toys of violence to children.

What are the goals of the campaign?

- Raise public awareness about the harmful ways toys of violence are marketed to children and how such toys contribute to the overall growth of violence in society.

- Create a community-wide effort to reduce the sale of violent toys and decrease other factors that contribute to violence in the lives of children.

- Develop activities that promote nonviolence and peaceful conflict resolution as an alternative to the violence marketed to children.

What is the Toy-Gun Buy-Back Program?

Two local toy stores are sponsoring a toy gun swap.

- Sandy & Son is offering a certificate (equal to a percentage of the value of the gun brought in) good toward the purchase of a nonviolent toy.

- Henry Bear's Park is offering to let children choose from a shelf of nonviolent toys in exchange for guns they bring in.

What else is the campaign doing?

Our activities include sponsoring public educational forums, developing early childhood peace-education curriculum for schools, and working with other groups in the city on violence prevention. Students from Lesley College have been trained to visit classrooms and talk to children about toys of violence and violence prevention issues. We continue to develop and expand our plans.

What can you do?

- Help children you know become involved in the Toy-Gun Buy-Back Program.

- Work to change how toys of violence are marketed to children, especially through mass-market toy stores and violent children's media.

- Contact us for more information.

Contact the Lion and Lamb Project (see Appendix C and the Resources section) for materials to help your community organize a violent toy trade-in.

Build coalitions with other professional, community, and other groups in your area.

The more various groups can pool their efforts in dealing with the problems in the media culture, the more effective everyone's efforts will be. For instance, look to your local early childhood professional and parent-teacher organizations, church groups, state attorney general's office, medical and pediatricians' organizations, education and public health departments.

Work to reduce the quantity and quality of the hazards of media culture in the wider society.

Voice your concerns and propose positive actions to government officials and policymakers. For example, if you see something on TV or in the media that you think is inappropriate for children, file a complaint with the Federal Communications Commission, the government agency responsible for overseeing media. Address your letters to

Federal Communications Commission
1919 M Street, NW
Washington, DC 20554

Include the following information in your complaint:

- call letters of the TV station (e.g., WXYZ, Channel 123)

- city/region in which you viewed the program
- brief description of the material you found offensive
- a request to keep your letter on file to be used when the station's broadcast license comes up for renewal (ask to contacted when license renewal is being considered).

Send a copy of your complaint to TV station or other companies involved.

Use the addresses and phone numbers in the Resources section and in your local phone book to voice your opinions (both positive and negative). Copy and distribute this information to other teachers, parents, and the wider community. You also can form community action groups to coordinate letter-writing and telephone efforts.

Express your concerns (as well as positive reactions) to those responsible for creating the media culture. You can contact local TV stations, national networks, local movie theaters, toy and video stores, and media producers who provide media programming and products to children in your area. Other groups that should hear your comments and concerns are manufacturers of media-linked toys and other products on shows that you find inappropriate or offensive or advertisers who have offensive ads. The following sample letter can give you an idea of how to frame your concerns.

Sample Letter to Broadcaster or Toy Company/Store

Dear [TV Broadcaster/Toy Company President/Toy Store Manager]:

I recently [watched an episode of _____ /shopped at _____]. I found [this program/specific toy/etc.] inappropriate for my child/children because [describe what offended you and why].

As [an educator/a parent], I am deeply concerned about the escalating violence in our country and the role that your [program/product/etc.] plays in promoting it. I will tell at least 10 others about my concerns with your [program/product] and urge them protect their children from it.

I hope you share my concerns about violence [etc.] and children. I urge you to play your role in helping to reduce the epidemic of violence in homes, schools, and the wider society by reducing the violence in [your program/products/etc.] and by investing your resources in [media/toys/etc.] that promote the healthy development of children.

And here is another example of a letter. A teacher wrote to a company that advertised heavily on children's TV programs that she found to be particularly violent.

Company Executive
Address of Company

Dear _____:

As a teacher of young children, I am deeply concerned that your company is heavily advertising its products during many children's programs that are extremely violent, such as *The Mighty Morphin Power Rangers* and *Batman.*

Educators, parents, and professional groups—such as the American Academy of Pediatrics, the American Medical Association, the National Association for the Education of Young Children, and the National Association of Attorneys General—have come out deploring the high amount of violence children are exposed to daily on children's television programs. These organizations cite a growing body of research showing that media violence contributes to violent attitudes and behaviors in children.

All Americans must take seriously the wake-up call coming from these organizations. We all must play our part in finding responsible and expeditious solutions to the problems created for children and society by media violence.

I am asking that you review your company's advertising policies. Please consider that children's minds as well as their bodies require nourishment. We need the help of your company to provide high-quality television to young children and to stop supporting programs that present and glorify gratuitous violence.

Use the media in your community to voice your ideas and concerns about what is happening around children's media and related issues. Write letters to the editor about specific media issues that come up in your community. Get other concerned members of your community to write letters too. If you know supporters of these efforts who have the skills to do so, get them to write editorial/commentary pieces for local newspapers. The letter that follows provides one example of the kind of issue you can write about. It was written by a parent after an unfortunate family movie outing.

To the Editor:

I recently took my 5-year-old son to the animated movie, [name of movie]. I decided to take him after reading a very favorable review in your paper in which the movie was described as "good, clean family fun."

I found the movie neither clean nor fun. There were many violent scenes. The adults in the movie were made to look like fools. And the children exhibited mean-spirited and racist behavior toward others. Throughout, my son kept asking me why the main characters (children) kept doing such mean things.

I have been hearing about more and more studies that show the negative effects media can have on children. We parents are told it is our job to decide what media is appropriate and not appropriate for our children. I try very hard to take this job seriously. I rely on the reviews in your newspaper to help me do it. You have let me down. How many other parents were also misled by your review?

I hope that in the future you will find reviewers who have the knowledge and sensitivity that it takes to review movies with the best interests of children and their families at heart.

Encourage local print and electronic media in your area to write stories about what your group is doing to combat the hazards of media culture. Find out which media people in your area are most sympathetic to the issues you raise (perhaps by the stories they already report) and try to establish an ongoing relationship with them. (I have found that they are often the people who have young children themselves!)

ACTION IDEA

When your group is planning some special activity (like a TV turn-off week), send simple press releases to those media people you think will be interested in covering the event.

When an upcoming media event may have a negative impact on children—like the opening of a violent movie—prepare materials for parents about your concerns and offer suggestions about what to do.

ACTION IDEA

Contact your local media to let them know about your concerns. Send them the materials you have prepared.

Here is an example of a letter to parents that was prepared when *The Mighty Morphin Power Rangers* movie came out in the summer of 1995. Teachers for Resisting Unhealthy Children's Entertainment (TRUCE) distributed it to parents around the country through early childhood educational settings.

Take Action to Protect Your Child from
The Mighty Morphin Power Rangers Movie

As teachers, we are worried about how *The Mighty Morphin Power Rangers* movie will affect your child. We have already been dealing with the problems the Power Ranger TV show has created in our classrooms. We have seen the negative ways the Power Rangers are affecting children's learning and their ideas about the world. We no longer can tolerate children's "entertainment" that depicts violence as the way to solve problems and whose ultimate purpose is to make huge profits, not to promote the well-being of children. We urge you to take a stand against the Power Ranger (PR) movie and toys and to work to lessen the negative impact the movie can have on your child.

Why are teachers concerned about the Power Ranger movie?

- In a national survey, more than 90% of teachers blamed Power Rangers for causing increased levels of classroom violence.

- A recent study found that children, after viewing one episode of the PR TV show, committed 7 times as many acts of aggression in play as children who didn't see the show.

- The PR TV show is the most violent children's show ever—with more than 100 acts of violence per episode, compared with fewer than 50 on the Ninja Turtles. (When do we say enough is enough and draw the line?)

- In 1994 the sale of toys and products with the PR logo surpassed $1 billion, an industry record.

- In New Zealand the PR TV program was taken off the air because of complaints from parents and teachers about the level of violence and how it was affecting children.

What can parents do?

The Power Rangers are very seductive for many children. Figuring out how to deal with the PR movie and toys can be a difficult challenge. Here are some suggestions to help you get started.

CONSIDER A BOYCOTT, especially for children under 6 who tend to focus more on the fighting than plots and have a hard time sorting out what is real and pretend. By boycotting, you will be taking a stand against marketing violence to children and helping to ensure there won't be a Power Ranger II movie! Here are some ideas to help you with a boycott:

- **Talk about your reasons** for boycotting the movie without making your child feel guilty for wanting to see it. It's important to let children say what they think too, even if they disagree with you.

- **Come up with an appealing alternative activity** to do in place of the movie.

- **Find other parents** who are willing to participate in a movie ban so that your child has a "support group" and sees that parents are working to make the world a safer place for children.

- **Get your child's school involved.** Community efforts can help children feel part of a powerful effort.

- **Write a letter or make a phone call** with your child to tell local theaters and newspapers about the stand you have taken. This can help children feel that their sacrifice is important and makes a difference.

IF YOU DECIDE TO SEE THE MOVIE, you can lessen its impact by

- **talking with your child in advance** about such things as what you both expect to see, what is real and what is not, what you think you will and won't like.

- **talking about the movie afterwards.** Help your child work through the content of the movie, especially the violence. For example, try asking, "Are the Power Rangers real or not? How could they have solved their problem without fighting?

WHETHER OR NOT YOUR CHILD SEES THE MOVIE:

- **Help your child resist the pull of PR toys and products.** Stores will be bulging with highly seductive PR products. The desire for them can create much stress. Work out with your child in advance about what you will or will not buy. Avoid impulse buying.

- **Keep open channels of communication about the Power Rangers.** No matter what you do, the movie hype will be present all around you. Talk to children about what they see or hear to continue to build ideas that counteract the negative messages of the movie.

- **Keep on the lookout for signs of Power Rangers** entering your child's life—in violent play or conversation. This can give you clues of things to talk about together.

- **Work with your child's teachers** to develop other strategies to combat media violence.

From remote control to social responsibilty

The degree to which a society can survive and thrive depends, to a great extent, on the degree to which it can support parents in their challenging task of raising children to become healthy, contributing members of that society. But increasingly, instead of supporting parents with these efforts, the media culture that surrounds children growing up today has created a society that does just the opposite. More and more, being a good parent means resisting the popular and media culture that society has allowed to be created for its children. And as a result, the job of parenting is made even harder—as are the jobs of all adults who care for children.

Understandably, the magnitude of the problem often leads adults to try to avoid dealing with the media culture as much as possible. The result is a too-frequent withdrawal from our rightful role in helping children learn to deal with the media culture that surrounds them. It prevents us from working together to create a media environment that can better support our efforts with children and for the best interests of society. We often give too much of a free rein to the media and media culture industries to influence our children by remote control.

We all have a vital role to play in creating a healthy media culture for children. Various constituencies assign the responsibility for dealing with the problems to different places. For instance, the media and toy industries generally say it is parents' responsiblity to control the media culture in their children's lives, putting as much of the burden as possible on parents. And many who focus on teaching media literacy to children put much of the responsibility on children themselves. They believe that arming children with the knowledge to "read" media and its messages is the best way to solve the problem. While each of these strategies has merit, no one of them on its own is sufficient to combat the hazards of contemporary media culture.

The responsibility for dealing with the media culture rests with everyone, as this book argues. This is the conclusion reached by many of the groups and individuals focusing on the well-being of children in our electronic age. Today, more than ever before, we see that action is needed at every level to protect children from the fallout of media culture and to create a media environment that serves the best interests of children, parents, teachers, and, ultimately, all of society.

NOTES

Introduction

1. To the school's credit, it recently has begun to develop a comprehensive and innovative media literacy program throughout the school community. The program, which will serve as a model of what the role of schools can be, has helped inform the content of this book.

Chapter 1

2. See J. Federman, *National Television Violence Study, Executive Summary, Volume 2* (Santa Barbara: Center for Communication and Social Policy, University of California, 1997), p. 25.

3. Unless otherwise indicated, the facts and figures in this section are from J. Murphy and K. Tucker, *Stay Tuned: Raising Media-Savvy Kids in the Age of the Channel-Surfing Couch Potato* (New York: Doubleday, 1996).

4. From K. Montgomery, *"Creating an Electronic Legacy for Our Children,"* paper presented at the annual meeting of Aspen Institute, Miami, February 1997.

5. For more information, see N. Carlsson-Paige and D. Levin, *Who's Calling the Shots? How to Respond Effectively to Children's Fascination with War Play, War Toys, and Violent TV* (Gabriola Island, B.C.: New Society, 1990).

6. See A. Marks, "Sexual Images: TV and Toy Trend Affects Young Children," *Christian Science Monitor,* 7 May 1996, pp. 1, 12.

7. See T. Grier, "R-rated Alien Bugs Your Child Will Beg to See. The Toys are PG. The Movie Definitely Isn't," *U.S. News and World Report* 10 November 1997, p. 75.

8. The facts and figures in the chart also come from A. Diamant, "Media Violence," *Parents Magazine* (October 1994), pp. 40–41, 45; M. Hickey, "How the Power Rangers Stole Christ-

mas," *Ladies Home Journal* (December 1995), pp. 125–26, 167, 169; *Playthings* (April 1994); J. Murphy and K. Tucker, *Stay Tuned: Raising Media-Savvy Kids in the Age of the Channel-Surfing Couch Potato* (New York: Doubleday, 1996); D. Levin and N. Carlsson-Paige, "The Mighty Morphin Power Rangers: Teachers Voice Concern," *Young Children* 50, no. 6 (1995), pp. 38–44; and J. Seabrook, "Why Is The Force Still with Us?" *The New Yorker* (January 1997), pp. 40–53.

9. See Carnegie Corporation of New York, *Years of Promise: A Comprehensive Learning Strategy for America's Children* (New York: Author, 1996).

10. For instance, see R. Slaby et al., *Early Violence Prevention: Tools for Teachers of Young Children* (Washington, D.C.: NAEYC, 1995); American Psychological Association, *Violence and Youth: Psychology's Response, Volume 1, Summary Report* (Washington, D.C.: Author, 1993); and A. Huston et al., *Big World, Small Screen: The Role of Television in American Society* (Lincoln: University of Nebraska Press, 1992).

11. About 125,000 youths under 18 years of age were arrested in 1994 for violent crimes (Children's Defense Fund, *The State of America's Children Yearbook 1996* (Washington, D.C.: Author, 1996).

12. One survey found that 70% of 7- to 10-year-olds worry about getting stabbed or shot at home or school (Children Now, news release, 6 December 1995).

13. See, for example, D. Levin and N. Carlsson-Paige, "The Mighty Morphin Power Rangers: Teachers Voice Concern," *Young Children* 50 (September 1995), pp. 38–44.

14. See D. Levin, "Play with Violence: Understanding and Responding Effectively" in *Play from Birth to Twelve: Contexts, Perspectives, and Meanings,* eds. D. Fromberg and D. Bergen (New York: Garland, in press); and N. Carlsson-Paige and D. Levin, *Who's Calling the Shots? How to Respond Effectively to Children's Fascination with War Play, War Toys, and Violent TV* (Gabriola Island, B.C.: New Society, 1990).

15. This idea comes from the American Medical Association, *Physician Guide to Media Violence* (Chicago: Author, 1996).

16. For instance, see N. Carlsson-Paige and D. Levin, *Who's Calling the Shots? How to Respond Effectively to Children's Fascination with War Play, War Toys, and Violent TV* (Gabriola Island, B.C.: New Society, 1990); J. Garbarino, *Raising Children in a Socially Toxic Environment* (San Francisco: Jossey-Bass, 1995); L. Coco, *Ralph Nader Presents: Children First! A Parent's Guide to Fighting Corporate Predators* (Washington, D.C.: Corporate Accountability Research Group, 1996); and D. Walsh, *Selling Out America's Children: How America Puts Profits Before Values—And What Parents Can Do* (Minneapolis: Fairview, 1994).

17. For more information about government policy and regulation, contact the Center for Media Education, 1511 K St., NW, Suite 518, Washington, DC 20005; 202-628-2620; Website http://tap.epn.org/cme.

18. For instance, see G. Gerbner, "The Ratings Rant, V-Chip Gyp, and TV Violence Shuffle: What Are the Real Issues?" *The Philadelphia Inquirer,* 30 January 1997.

19. For free copies of *TV Parental Guidelines,* a pamphlet summary of the TV ratings system, write TV Parental Guidelines, P.O. Box 14097, Washington, DC 20004; or visit the Website at http://www.tvguidelines.org.

20. For information about efforts to establish government policies regarding children and the Internet, contact the Center for Media Education, 1511 K St., NW, Suite 518, Washington, DC 20005; 202-628-2620; Website http://tap.epn.org/cme.

21. Published by the Coalition for Quality Children's Media, 535 Cordova Road, Suite 456, Santa Fe, NM 87501; 505-989-8076; Website http://www.cqcm.org/kids/first.

22. For more information, contact Ready-to-Learn Service, Public Broadcasting System, 1320 Braddock Place, Alexandria, VA 22314; 703-739-5000; Website http://www.pbs.org.

23. See *InfoActive Kids: A Field Guide to the Children's Television Act* (Washington, D.C.: Center for Media Education, Summer 1997).

Chapter 2

24. For instance, see J. Federman, *National Television Violence Study, Executive Summary, Volume 2* (Santa Barbara: Center for Communication and Social Policy, University of California, 1997).

Chapter 4

25. The dialogue is adapted from D. Levin, "Speaking of Superheroes," *Scholastic Early Childhood Today* (November/December 1994), pp. 54–56.

26. For more detailed help on teaching peaceful conflict resolution, see N. Carlsson-Paige and D. Levin, *Before Push Comes to Shove: Building Conflict-Resolution Skills with Young Children* (St. Paul, Minn.: Redleaf, in press).

27. This is also an issue with the growth of World Wide Web advertising as unidentified features of Websites. For more information, contact the Center for Media Education (see the Resources).

28. For instance, see D. Kunkel and D. Roberts, "Young Minds and the Marketplace Values: Issues in Children's Television Advertising," *Journal of Social Issues* 47 no. 1 (1991), pp. 57–72.

29. For more information on making and using curriculum webs, see D. Levin, "Weaving Curriculum Webs: Planning, Guiding, and Recording Curriculum Activities," *Early Care and Education* (Summer 1986), pp. 16–19; and S. Workman and M. Anziano, "Curriculum Webs: Weaving Connections from Children to Teachers," *Young Children* 48 no. 2 (1993), pp. 4–9.

Chapter 5

30. For instance, see K. Averill-Savino, "T. Berry Brazelton Talks about '90's Parents and Their Kids," *Sacramento Parent Magazine* (January 1997), pp. 17, 19.

31. For a more complete discussion of the developmental issues underlying children's understanding of consumerism and strategies for responding, see N. Carlsson-Paige and D. Levin, *Who's Calling the Shots? How to Respond Effectively to Children's Fascination with War Play, War Toys, and Violent TV* (Gabriola Island, B.C.: New Society, 1990).

Chapter 6

32. Adapted from D. Levin and N. Carlsson-Paige, "Contemporary Toys as a Social Problem," in *Encyclopedia of Childhood*, eds. D. King and B. Rothman (New York: Henry Holt Reference, in press).

33. For a more complete discussion on the influences of media and media violence on play, see N. Carlsson-Paige and D. Levin, *Who's Calling the Shots? How to Respond Effectively to Children's Fascination with War Play, War Toys, and Violent TV* (Gabriola Island, B.C.: New Society, 1990); D. Levin, "Play with Violence: Understanding and Responding Effectively" in *Play from Birth to Twelve: Contexts, Perspectives, and Meanings*, eds. D. Fromberg and D. Bergen (New York: Garland, in press); and D. Levin, "Endangered Play, Endangered Development: A Constructivist View of the Role of Play in Development and Learning," in *Playing for Keeps*, ed. A. Phillips (St. Paul, Minn.: Redleaf, 1996).

Chapter 7

34. Teachers and parents report having similar unexpected, disoriented experiences with the sexual content children see in the media. Most of what is talked about in this chapter regarding violence is also relevant to helping children deal with the sexual content they hear about in the news.

35. For more information on helping children deal with the violence in their lives, see J. Garbarino et al., *Children in Danger: Dealing with the Effects of Community Violence* (San Francisco: Jossey-Bass, 1992); and D. Levin, *Teaching Young Children in Violent Times: Building a Peaceable Classroom* (Cambridge, Mass.: Educators for Social Responsibility, 1994).

36. For one teacher's account of how she did this, see J. Danielson, "Controversial Issues and Young Children: Kindergartners Try to Understand Chernobyl," in *Promising Practices in Teaching Social Responsibility*, eds. S. Berman and P. LaFarge (Albany: State University of New York Press, 1993).

37. Being "used to it" is not a relevant criterion for deciding what is and is not appropriate content for children. Children can become desensitized to violent and scary content. In cases in which children are not scared by extreme content, we should be *more* concerned, because being distressed often is an appropriate response.

38. For more information, see N. Carlsson-Paige and D. Levin, *Before Push Comes to Shove: Building Conflict Resolution Skills with Children* (St. Paul, Minn.: Redleaf, in press); and D. Levin, *Teaching Young Children in Violent Times: Building a Peaceable Classroom* (Cambridge, Mass.: Educators for Social Responsibility, 1994).

Chapter 10

39. For a more detailed discussion of media-linked toys and play, see N. Carlsson-Paige and D. Levin, *Who's Calling the Shots? How to Respond Effectively to Children's Fascination with War Play, War Toys, and Violent TV* (Gabriola Island, B.C.: New Society, 1990).

Chapter 11

40. From K. Averill-Savino, "T. Berry Brazelton Talks about '90's Parents and Their Kids," *Sacramento Parent Magazine* (January 1997): 17, 19.

RESOURCES

Bibliography

American Medical Association, *Physician Guide to Media Violence* (Chicago: Author, 1996).

American Psychological Association, *Violence and Youth: Psychology's Response, Vol. 1, Summary Report* (Washington, D.C.: Author, 1993).

Bennett, S., and R. Bennett, *Kick the TV Habit! A Simple Program for Changing Your Family's Television Viewing* (New York: Penguin, 1994).

Boyatzis, C., "Why Worry about the Mighty Morphin Power Rangers?" *Young Children* 53 no. 1 (1997): 76–81.

Cain, B., and C. Bohrer, "Battling Jurassic Park: From a Fascination with Violence Toward Constructive Knowledge," *Young Children* 53 no. 1 (1997): 73–75.

Carlsson-Paige, N., and D. Levin, *The War Play Dilemma: Balancing Needs and Values in the Early Childhood Classroom* (New York: Teachers College Press, 1987).

Carlsson-Paige, N., and D. Levin, *Who's Calling the Shots? How to Respond Effectively to Children's Fascination with War Play, War Toys, and Violent TV* (Gabriola Island, B.C.: New Society, 1990).

Carlsson-Paige, N., and D. Levin, "Making Peace in Violent Times: A Constructivist Approach to Conflict Resolution," *Young Children* 48 no. 1 (1992): 4–13.

Carlsson-Paige, N., and D. Levin, *Teaching Conflict Resolution to Young Children: Building a Foundation Through Literature* (St. Paul, Minn.: Redleaf, 1998).

Carlsson-Paige, N., and D. Levin, *Before Push Comes to Shove: Building Conflict-Resolution Skills with Children* (St. Paul, Minn.: Redleaf, in press).

Carnegie Corporation of New York, *Years of Promise: A Comprehensive Learning Strategy for America's Children* (New York: Author, 1996).

Center for Media Education, *Connecting Children to the Future: A Telecommunications Policy Guide for Child Advocates* (Washington, D.C.: Author, 1996).

Center for Media Education, *Web of Deception: Threats to Children from Online Marketing* (Washington, D.C.: Author, 1996).

Center for Media Literacy, *Parenting in a TV Age: A Media Literacy Workshop Kit on Children and Television* (Los Angeles: Author, 1991).

Cesarone, B., "Video Games and Children," *ERIC Digest* (January 1994).

Chen, M., *The Smart Parent's Guide to Kids' TV* (San Francisco: KQED, 1994).

Children Now, News release, 6 December 1995.

Childrens Defense Fund, *The State of America's Children Yearbook 1996* (Washington, D.C.: Author, 1996).

Coalition for Quality Children's Media, *Kids First! Directory: A Consumer's Guide to Quality Children's Videos and CD-ROMs*, 2d ed. (Santa Fe, N.M.: Author, 1996).

Coco, L., *Ralph Nader Presents: Children First! A Parent's Guide to Fighting Corporate Predators* (Washington, D.C.: Corporate Accountability Research Group, 1996).

Considine, D., G. Haley, and L. Lacy, *Imagine That: Developing Critical Thinking and Critical Viewing through Children's Literature* (Englewood, Colo.: Teacher Ideas, 1994).

Danielson, J.B., "Controversial Issues and Young Children: Kindergartners Try to Understand Chernobyl," in *Promising Practices in Teaching Social Responsibility,* eds. S. Berman and P. LaFarge (Albany: State University of New York Press, 1993).

DeGaetano, G., and K. Bander, *Screen Smarts: Raising Media Literate Kids* (Boston: Houghton Mifflin, 1996).

Diamont, A., "Media Violence," *Parents Magazine* (October 1994): 40–45.

Dines, G., and J. Humez, eds., *Gender, Race and Class in Media: A Text-Reader* (Thousand Oaks, Calif.: Sage, 1995).

Douglas, S., *Where the Girls Are: Growing Up Female with the Mass Media* (New York: Time Books, 1994).

Farish, J., *When Disaster Strikes: Helping Young Children Cope* (Washington, D.C.: NAEYC, 1995 [brochure]).

Federman, J., ed., *National Television Violence Study, Executive Summary, Volume 2* (Santa Barbara: Center for Communication and Social Policy, University of California, 1997).

Federman, J., *Media Ratings: Design, Use and Consequences* (Studio City, Calif.: Mediascope, 1996).

Fox, R., *Harvesting Minds: How TV Commercials Control Kids* (Westport, Conn.: Greenwood, 1997).

Garbarino, J., *Raising Children in a Socially Toxic Environment* (San Francisco: Jossey-Bass, 1995).

Garbarino, J., N. Dubrow, K. Kostelny, and C. Pardo, *Children in Danger: Dealing with the Effects of Community Violence* (San Francisco: Jossey-Bass, 1992).

Gerber, G., "The Ratings Rant, V-chip Gyp, and TV Violence Shuffle: What Are the Real Issues?" *Philadelphia Inquirer*, 30 January 1997.

Greenfield, P., and R. Codking, eds., *Interacting with Video* (Norwood, N.J.: Ablex, 1996).

Gronlund, G., "Coping with Ninja Turtle Play in My Kindergarten Classroom," *Young Children* 48 no. 1 (1992): 21–25.

Hesse, P., and D. Poklemba, *Rambo Meets Care Bears: Responding to Children's Television in the Classroom* (Cambridge, Mass.: Center for Psychology and Social Change, 1994).

Healy, J., *Endangered Minds: Why Children Don't Think and What We Can Do about It* (New York: Touchstone, 1990).

Hickey, M., "How the Power Rangers Stole Christmas," *Ladies Home Journal* 112 (December 1995): 126, 167, 169.

Horton, J., and J. Zimmer, *Media Violence and Children: A Guide for Parents* (Washington, D.C.: NAEYC, 1994 [brochure]).

Huston, A., *Big World, Small Screen: The Role of Television in American Society* (Lincoln: University of Nebraska Press, 1992).

Kilpatrick, W., G. Wolfe, and S. Wolfe, *The Family New Media Guide: A Parent's Guide to the Very Best Choices in Values-Oriented Media* (New York: Touchstone, 1997).

Kinder, M., *Playing with Power in Movies, Television, and Video Games: From Muppet Babies to Teenage Mutant Ninja Turtles* (Berkeley: University of California, 1991).

Kline, S., *Out of the Garden: Toys and Children's Culture in the Age of TV Marketing* (New York: Verso, 1993).

Kunkel, D., and D. Roberts, "Young Minds and Marketplace Values: Issues in Children's Television Advertising," *Journal of Social Issues* 47 no. 1 (1991): 57–72.

Levin, D., *Teaching Young Children in Violent Times: Building a Peaceable Classroom* (Cambridge, Mass.: Educators for Social Responsibility, 1994).

Levin, D., "Endangered Play, Endangered Development: A Constructivist View of the Role of Play in Development and Learning," in *Playing for Keeps*, ed. A. Phillips (St. Paul, Minn.: Redleaf, 1996).

Levin, D., "Play with Violence: Understanding and Responding Effectively," in *Play from Birth to Twelve: Contexts, Perspectives, and Meanings*, eds. Fromberg and D. Berger (New York: Garland, 1997).

Levin, D., and N. Carlsson-Paige, "Developmentally Appropriate Television: Putting Children First," *Young Children* 49 no. 5 (1994): 38–44.

Levin, D., and N. Carlsson-Paige, "The Mighty Morphin Power Rangers: Teachers Voice Concern," *Young Children* 50 no. 6 (1995): 67–72.

Levin, D., and N. Carlsson-Paige, "Contemporary Toys as a Social Problem," in *Encyclopedia of Childhood*, eds. D. King and B. Rothman (New York: Henry Holt Reference, in press).

Levine, M., *Viewing Violence: How Media Violence Affects Your Child's and Adolescent's Development* (New York: Doubleday, 1996).

McDonnell, K., *Kid Culture: Children and Adults and Popular Culture* (Toronto: Second Story, 1994).

Mediascope, Inc., *National Television Violence Study: Executive Summary 1994–95* (Studio City, Calif.: Author, n.d.).

Miller, B., S. O'Connor, S. Sirignano, and P. Joshi, *"I Wish Kids Didn't Watch So Much TV": Out-of-school Time in Three Low-income Communities* (Wellesley, Mass.: Wellesley College Center for Research on Women, 1996).

Minnow, N., and C. Lamay, *Abandoned in the Wasteland: Children, Television, and the First Amendment* (New York: Hill & Wang, 1995).

Montgomery, K., "Creating an Electronic Legacy for Our Children" paper presented at Aspen Institute Conference, 14–17 February 1997, Miami, Fla.

Murphy, J., and K. Tucker, *Stay Tuned: Raising Media-savvy Kids in the Age of the Channel-surfing Couch Potato* (New York: Doubleday, 1996).

National Association for the Education of Young Children, "NAEYC Position Statement on Media Violence in Children's Lives," *Young Children* 45 no. 5 (1990): 18–21. (See Appendix A.)

National Association for the Education of Young Children, "NAEYC Position Statement on Violence in the Lives of Children," *Young Children* 48 no. 6 (1993): 80–84. (Also available in brochure form.)

Papert, S., *The Connected Family: Bridging the Digital Generation Gap* (Atlanta: Longstreet, 1996).

Parry, A., "Children Surviving in a Violent World—Choosing Nonviolence," *Young Children* 48 no. 6 (1993): 13–15.

Provenzo, E., *Video Kids: Making Sense of Nintendo* (Cambridge, Mass.: Harvard University Press, 1991).

Ready at Five Partnership, *Moving Young Children's Play Away from TV Violence: A How-to Guide for Early Childhood Educators* (Baltimore: Author, n.d.).

Rogers, F., and H.B. Sharapan, "Helping Parents, Teachers, and Caregivers Deal with Children's Concerns about War," *Young Children* 46 no. 3 (1991): 12–13.

Seabrook, J., "Why Is The Force Still with Us?" *New Yorker* (January 1997): 40–53.

Sheff, D., *Game Over: How Nintendo Conquered the World* (New York: Vintage, 1994).

Seiter, E., *Sold Separately: Parents and Children in Consumer Culture* (New Brunswick, N.J.: Rutgers University Press, 1993).

Slaby, R., W. Roedell, D. Arezzo, and K. Hendrix, *Early Violence Prevention: Tools for Teachers of Young Children* (Washington, D.C.: NAEYC, 1995).

Stern, S., and T. Schoenhaus, *Toyland: The High-stakes Game of the Toy Industry* (Chicago: Contemporary, 1990).

Viewpoint (N. Carlsson-Paige and D. Levin, "Can Teachers Help Resolve the War-Play Dilemma?"; J. Greenberg, "Making Friends with the Power Rangers"; B. Klemm, "Video Game Violence"; J. Kuyendall, "Is Gun Play OK Here?") *Young Children* 50 no. 5 (1995): 53–63.

Wallach, L.B., "Helping Children Cope with Violence," *Young Children* 48 no. 4 (1993): 4–11.

Walsh, D., *Selling out America's Children: How America Puts Profits Before Values—And What Parents Can Do* (Minneapolis, Minn.: Fairview, 1994).

Wright, J., and D. Shade, eds., *Young Children: Active Learners in a Technological Age* (Washington, D.C.: NAEYC, 1994).

Selected Videos on Media Violence and Children

KQED, *The Smart Parent's Guide to TV Violence* (San Francisco: KQED-Public Broadcasting System and National PTA, 1996).

DeGaetano, G., *Television and Video: Children at Risk* (Redmond, Wash.: Train of Thought, 1995).

Gerbner, G., *The Killing Screens: Media and the Culture of Violence* (Northhampton, Mass.: Foundation for Media Education, 1994).

Hesse, P., *The World Is a Dangerous Place* (Cambridge, Mass.: Center for Psychology and Social Change, 1989).

Walsh, D., *Unplug Your Kids* (Minneapolis, Minn.: National Institute on Media and the Family, 1996).

Selected Children's Books with Annotations

To Facilitate Discussions about TV and Media

Bourgeois, P., *Franklin's Bad Day* (New York: Scholastic, 1997).

By talking things over with his dad, Franklin learns how to deal with his angry and sad feelings.

Brown, M., *Arthur's TV Trouble* (New York: Little Brown, 1995).

Arthur learns the hard way that the products advertised on TV are not always as they seem.

Brown, M., and L.K. Brown, *The Bionic Bunny Show* (New York: Little Brown, 1984).

Wilbur, a rabbit actor, is the star of a TV show about a bunny with superhero qualities. The real-life Wilbur, however, suffers bumps and bruises as the program's director asks him to perform bionic-like feats.

Dahl, L., *James and the Giant Peach: The Book and Movie Scrapbook* (New York: Disney Press, 1996).

Roald Dahl's daughter talks about her father's life, including how the movie of his famous book was made. Not for preschoolers.

Denholtz, R., *The Day the TV Broke* (January Productions, 1986).

When their TV breaks, Jose and Maria invite their friends to create their own TV shows and commercials using puppets, music, and dance.

Dupasquier, P., *No More Television!* (London: Anderson, 1995).

The Dixon family loves to watch TV, but when Mr. Dixon realizes just how much TV the family watches, he plans several schemes to cut back.

Gibbons, G., *Lights! Camera! Action! How a Movie Is Made* (New York: Crowell, 1985).

A step-by-step description of how a movie is made, from the writing of the script, casting, and rehearsing to filming, editing, and showing.

Hankin, R., *What Was It Like Before Television?* (Austin, Tex.: Steck-Vaughn, 1995).

An older woman explains to her younger friends how much fun she had as a child without TV. She describes play-acting, collecting stamps, singing, playing musical instruments, sewing, and playing board games.

McPhail, D., *Fix-It* (New York: Dutton Children's Books, 1984).

When Emma Bear's TV breaks, her mother, father, and the TV-repair bear try to fix it. Meanwhile, Emma becomes so engrossed in other activities that, when the TV set is finally fixed, she doesn't even watch it.

Merbreier, W.C., *Television: What's Behind What You See* (New York: Farrar, Straus and Giroux, 1996).

This book is packed with information about all aspects of TV production, but it's best for elementary age children because it gets pretty complicated and detailed. Specific sections might be used when younger children raise particular questions.

Novak, M., *Mouse TV* (New York: Scholastic, 1994)

When the mouse family's TV breaks, they discover a whole new world of creative ways to spend time together.

Polacco, P., *Aunt Chip and the Great Triple Creek Dam Affair* (New York: Philomel, 1996).

With the help of her nephew, Aunt Chip saves a town in which everyone has forgotten how to read because of their complete devotion to TV.

Winn, C., and D. Walsh, *Box Head Boy* (Minneapolis, Minn.: Fairview, 1996).

When Denny's head becomes a TV set, he quickly learns that a life inside the tube is not as much fun as he thought it would be.

Ziefert, H., *When the TV Broke* (New York: Puffin, 1989).

When the TV goes on the blink, Jeffrey must find other things to do to keep busy. Then, when the TV set is repaired, Jeffrey has discovered something he'd rather do than watch TV.

For Older Children

Byars, B., *The TV Kid* (New York: Puffin, 1976).

A boy who loves to watch TV often daydreams about what he sees. One day his daydreams lead him to a real-life situation full of danger.

Cross, R., *Movie Magic: A Behind-the-Scenes Look at Filmmaking* (New York: Sterling, 1994).

Packed with facts, explanations, photographs, and drawings about how films are made, this is an excellent resource for helping older children sort out the difference between pretend and real.

Platt, R., *Film* (Toronto, Ont.: Stoddart, 1992).

While the text is quite advanced for primary-age children, this a useful reference book, full of intriguing information and photographs about the history of filmmaking and offering a detailed look at a film set.

Rodgers, M., *A Billion for Boris* (New York: Harper Trophy, 1974).

When a rewired TV starts getting tomorrow's programs today, should the discovery be used for the good of humanity or to make a fortune?

Scott, E., *Look Alive: Behind the Scenes of an Animated Film* (New York: Morrow Junior, 1992).

A high-quality, serious look at the entire process of making an animated movie. Some photos and illustrations but a lot of text. Very useful when older children really want to explore the animation process.

Spinelli, J., *The Library Card* (New York: Scholastic, 1997).

During TV Turn-off Week, a mysterious library card opens up wonderful new possibilities for the children (animals) who found it.

To Facilitate Teaching of Nonviolent Conflict Resolution

Carlsson-Paige, N., *The Best Day of the Week* (St. Paul, Minn.: Redleaf, 1998).

Calvin and Angela disagree about whether the card table they found in the trash should become a store or a pirate ship. The process they go through in solving their problem exemplifies the skills involved in peaceful conflict resolution.

Greenfield, E., *First Pink Light* (New York: Black Butterfly, 1976).

Mother and son negotiate a conflict in this poignant story about waiting for Daddy to come home.

Lionni, L., *Six Crows* (New York: Scholastic, 1988).

A farmer and six crows fight over the same wheat field until they learn the value of communication.

Piers, H., *Thunder Foot and Long Neck* (London: Puffin, 1982).

Two dinosaurs who are afraid of each other learn how to make beautiful music together.

Rosen, M., *This Is Our House* (Boston: Walker, 1996).

George wants to keep the cardboard-carton house all to himself, but the other children come up with the better solution. (Also helpful in facilitating play.)

To Facilitate Creative Play

Dobrin, A., *Josephine's Imagination* (New York: Scholastic, 1973).

When she has nothing to play with, Josephine follows a wise grown-up's advice and creates her own special broom doll.

Hutchins, P., *Changes, Changes* (New York: Macmillan, 1971).

Blocks can be one of the most exciting toys to play with when you use your imagination.

Keats, E.J., *Louie* (New York: Scholastic, 1975).

A puppet show has a big impact on Louie. Two other books about Louie, *The Trip* and *Regards to the Man on the Moon,* provide rich ideas for more dramatic play.

McLeran, A., *Roxanboxen* (New York: Puffin, 1991).

On a empty lot children create an imaginary world with boxes.

Martin, A., *Rachel Parker, Kindergarten Show-off* (New York: Scholastic, 1992).

Olivia thinks Rachel is nothing but a show-off, but through creative play the girls learn to get along.

Schermbrucker, R., *Charlie's House* (New York: Viking, 1991).

A South African boy, with no toys to play with or even a house to live in, creates a playhouse from cast-off materials.

Walsh, J., *Connie Came to Play* (New York: Puffin, 1997).

Robert doesn't want to share his toys when Connie comes to visit, so she uses her imagination to find her own way of playing. (Also good for working on conflict resolution.)

Organizations Working on Media and Media Violence Issues

American Academy of Pediatrics
Department C-TV
141 Northwest Point Boulevard
PO Box 927
Elk Grove Village, IL 60009
http://www.aap.org

Publishes position statements and informational booklets; co-sponsors *The Smart Parent's Campaign on Kids' TV* with the Public Broadcasting System.

American Medical Association
515 North State Street
Chicago, IL 60610
312-464-5563

Publishes *Physician Guide to Media Violence* ($3), an excellent overview of media violence research and action suggestions.

American Psychological Association
750 First Street
Washington, DC 20002
202-336-6046

Produces materials summarizing research findings on media violence.

Better Business Bureau
Children's Advertising Review Unit
845 3rd Avenue
New York, NY 10022
212-705-0123

Industry regulatory group that investigates complaints about TV ads.

Center for Media Education
1511 K Street, NW, Suite 518
Washington, DC 20005
202-628-2620
http://tap.epn.org/cme

Leads a national coalition of educational groups working to educate the public and promotes public policies to improve children's TV. Publishes *A Parent's Guide to Kids TV* and policy resource materials including *InfoActive Kids* (a newsletter-$35/year); *Connecting Children to the Future: A Telecommunications Policy Guide tor Child Advocates;* and *Web of Deception: Threats to Children from Online Marketing.*

Center for Media Literacy
4727 Wilshire Boulevard, Suite 403
Los Angeles, CA 90010
213-913-4177
http://www.medialit.org

Publishes media literacy materials, including the highly acclaimed curriculum *Beyond Blame.*

Children Now
1212 Broadway, 5th floor
Oakland, CA 94612
1-800-CHILD44
http://www.childrennow.org

Researches a wide range of children's issues and media concerns, advocates public policy, and promotes public education. Publishes accessible reports, including *Children, Values, and the Entertainment Media; The Reflection on the Screen: Television's Image of Children;* and *Sex, Kids, and the Family Home;* also publishes the useful guide *Talking with Children about Tough Issues* (including TV violence).

Coalition for Quality Children's Media
535 Cordova Road, Suite 456
Santa Fe, NM 87501
505-989-8076
http://www.cqcm.org/kidsfirst

Kids First! (a newsletter) rates and reviews children's videos; *Kids First! Directory* provides comprehensive information for choosing appropriate videos and CD-ROMs.

Cultural Environment Movement
3508 Market Street
Philadelphia, PA 19104
215-387-8034

A coalition of media literacy advocates working to counteract the negative effects of the media culture.

Families Against Violence Advocacy Network
Institute for Peace and Justice
4144 Lindell Boulevard, Suite 408
St. Louis, MO 63108
310-533-4445

Publishes *Families Creating a Circle of Peace: A Guide for Living the Family Pledge of Nonviolence* ($5).

Lion and Lamb Project
4300 Montgomery Avenue, Suite 104
Bethesda, MD 20814
301-654-3091

Parent group supports community efforts to promote healthy play and nonviolent toys; publishes comprehensive *Parent Action Kit* ($7.95).

Media Education Foundation
26 Center Street
Northampton, MA 01060
800-659-6882
http://www.igc.org/mef

Produces and disseminates media literacy resources, including videos for working with adults on media issues.

Media Scope
12711 Ventura Boulevard
Studio City, CA 01694
818-508-2080

Promotes positive social issues in media; serves as clearinghouse for media violence materials.

Mothers Offended by the Media (MOM)
PO Box 382
Southampton, MA 01073
413-536-9282

Raises public awareness about appropriate media for young children and for a more appropriate ratings system for young children's media; publishes newsletter.

National Alliance for Non-violent Programming
1864 Banking Street
Greensboro, NC
910-370-0407

Provides support, advocacy help, and education materials to help build community coalitions that teach media literacy and nonviolent problem solving.

National Association for the Education of Young Children
1509 16th Street, NW
Washington, DC 20036-1426
1-800-424-2460
http://www.naeyc.org/naeyc

Publishes position statements and brochures on media violence and young children and on violence in the lives of children.

National Coalition against TV Violence
5132 Newport Avenue
Bethesda, MD 20816
301-986-0362

Promotes public awareness of the problems created by media violence.

National Institute on Media and the Family
2450 Riverside Avenue
Minneapolis, MN 55454
800-672-5437
http://www.mediaandthefamily.org

Produces resources for parents for evaluating children's media, including the video *Unplug the Kids* and a newsletter.

National Parent Teachers Association
700 North Rush Street
Chicago, IL 60611
302-670-6783
http://www.pta.org

Offers packets and workshops on appropriate media use with children.

National Parental Guidelines
PO Box 14097
Washington, DC 20004
202-879-9364
http://www.tvguidelines.org

Prepares materials to keep parents informed about the TV ratings system to accompany the V-chip on new TV sets.

Public Broadcasting System's Ready to Learn Service
1320 Braddock Place
Alexandria, VA 22314
701-739-5000
http://www.pbs.org/learn/rtl

Oversees 40 hours a week of educational programming offerings on public television and provides resources for parents and child caregivers on how to use these programs as an educational tool; co-sponsor with the American Academy of Pediatrics of *The Smart Parent's Campaign on Kids' TV*.

Teachers for Resisting Unhealthy Children's Entertainment
PO Box 441261
West Somerville, MA 02144

Publishes materials for teachers and parents to help children resist violent toys and the media.

Television Project
11160 Veirs Mill Road
L-15 Suite 277
Wheaton, MD 20902
301-588-4001
http://www.tvp.org

Prepares materials and *Beyond TV* newsletter to raise awareness of the ways television affects families; promotes alternatives and strategies for controlling TV use.

TV-Free America
1322 18th Street, NW, Suite 300
Washington, DC 20036
202-887-0436

Organizes annual TV Turn-off Week; prepares materials for the event.

ACTION IDEA

Use your phone book to find the phone numbers of the network affiliate stations in your area and include them in the following list (on page 172). Then make a copy of the list and keep it next to your phone. Make extra copies and give it to parents and friends.

Get in the habit of calling on a regular basis to let stations know what programs you do and do not like.

National TV Networks

ABC Entertainment
2040 Avenue of the Stars
Century City, CA 90067
318-556-1401

Local phone # _____

CBS Audience Services
51 West 52nd Street
New York, NY 10019
212-975-4321

Local phone # _____

Discovery Channel
7700 Wisconsin Avenue, Suite 700
Bethesda, MD 20814
301-986-0444

Local phone # _____

Disney Channel
3800 West Almada Avenue
Burbank, CA 91505
818-569-7897

Local phone # _____

Fox Broadcast Studios
PO Box 900
Beverly Hills, CA 90213
310-277-2211

Local phone # _____

NBC Entertainment
30 Rockefeller Plaza
New York, NY 10020
212-664-4444

Local phone # _____

Nickelodeon
1515 Broadway
New York, NY 10036
212-258-7579

Local phone # _____

PBS
1320 Braddock Place
Alexandria, VA 223124
703-739-5000

Local phone # _____

TNT/Turner Network TV
1050 Techwood Drive, NW
Atlanta, GA 30318
404-885-4538

Local phone # _____

ACTION IDEA

Find the phone numbers of your state and local officials and fill the numbers in on the following list. Then copy it and place it next to your phone. Contact the appropriate officials when issues of concern arise, especially when policy and legislative issues regarding media and media violence are being considered.

Government Officials

Federal Communications Commission
Mass Media Complaints
1919 M Street, NW
Washington, DC 20554
202-418-1430

> Federal agency that regulates the television industry

Elected Officials

The White House
1600 Pennsylvania Avenue
Washington, DC 20500
202-456-1414
e-mail president@whitehouse.gov

U.S. Senator _____

Phone # _____

U.S. Senator _____

Phone # _____

U.S. Rep. _____

Phone # _____

Governor _____

Phone # _____

Major Toy Manufacturers and Retailers

Bandai America, Inc.
12851 East 166th Street
Cerritos, CA 90701
310-926-0947

> Products include Power Rangers and Sailor Moon action figures

Lewis Galoob Toys
500 Forbes Boulevard
South San Francisco, CA 94080
415-952-1678

> Products include Micro Machines, Sky Dancers, Ultra Force, Star Wars, and Pound Puppies

Hasbro Toy Group
1027 Newport Avenue
Pawtucket, RI 02862
401-431-8697

> Produces Batman, GI Joe, Godzilla, Mortal Kombat, Play-Doh, Star Wars, and Transformers. Also owns **Kenner, Playskool, Tonka**

Mattel Toys
333 Continental Boulevard
El Segundo, CA 90245
310-524-2000

> Producers of Barbie, Hot Wheels, and Pocahontas. Also owns **Tyco**

McFarlane Toys (Irwin Toys, Inc.)
11918 Farmington Road
Livonia, MI 48150
313-425-0340

> Producer of Spawn action figures based on the best-selling comic book

Nintendo of America
PO Box 957
Redmond, WA 98073
800-255-3700

Saban Entertainment
400 W. Alameda Avenue
Burbank, CA 91505
818-972-4800

> Creators of Power Rangers, Sailor Moon, VF Troopers, and more

Sega Enterprises
255 Shoreline Drive
Redwood City, CA 94065
414-508-2800

Toys R Us
461 From Road
Paramus, NJ 07652
201-262-7800

NAEYC POSITION STATEMENT ON MEDIA VIOLENCE IN CHILDREN'S LIVES

Adopted April 1990; reaffirmed July 1994

During the past decade, America has witnessed an alarming increase in the incidence of violence in the lives of children. On a daily basis, children in America are victims of violence, as witnesses to violent acts in their homes or communities, or as victims of abuse, neglect, or personal assault. The causes of violent behavior in society are complex and interrelated. Among the significant contributors are poverty, racism, unemployment, illegal drugs, inadequate or abusive parenting practices, and real-life adult models of violent problem-solving behavior. NAEYC, the nation's largest organization of early childhood professionals, is deeply concerned about the destructive effect of violent living conditions and experiences on many of our nation's children.

At the same time that there has been an increase in the number of reported violent acts directed at children, there has been an increase in the amount and severity of violent acts observed by children through the media, including television, movies, computer games, and videotapes, and an increase in the manufacture and distribution of weapon-like toys and other products directly linked to violent programming. NAEYC believes the trend toward increased depiction of violence in the media jeopardizes the healthy development of significant numbers of our nation's children.

In response, NAEYC's Governing Board appointed a panel of experts to guide the development of initiatives and resources to assist teachers and parents in confronting the issue of violence in the lives of children. This position statement addresses one aspect of the problem—media violence—and is the first in a series of projects the Association plans to address this important issue. We have chosen to address the issue of media violence first because, of all the sources and manifestations of violence in children's lives, it is perhaps the most easily corrected. The media industry ought to serve the public interest and ought to be subject to government regulation.

Position

NAEYC condemns violent television programming, movies, videotapes, computer games, and other forms of media directed to children. NAEYC believes that it is the responsibility of adults and of public policy to protect children from unnecessary and potentially harmful exposure to violence through the media and to protect children from television content and advertising practices that exploit their special vulnerability (Huston, Watkins, & Kunkel 1989). NAEYC believes that television and other media have the potential to be very effective educational tools for children. Research demonstrates that television viewing is a highly complex, cognitive activity, during which children are actively involved in learning (Anderson & Collins 1988). Therefore, NAEYC supports efforts to use media constructively to expand children's knowledge and promote the development of positive social values. NAEYC also supports measures that can be taken by responsible adults to limit children's exposure to violence through the media. Such efforts include but are not limited to:

• legislation requiring reinstatement of guidelines for children's television by the Federal Communication Commission, including requirements for videotapes and elimination of television programs linked to toys

• legislation limiting advertising on children's programming, and standards for toys to ensure that they are not only physically safe but also psychologically safe

• legislation enabling the development of voluntary television-industry standards to alleviate violence in programming, specifically exempting such efforts from anti-trust regulation

• promotion of more developmentally appropriate, educational programming that meets children's diverse needs for information, entertainment, aesthetic appreciation, positive role models, and knowledge about the world (Huston et al. 1989)

• development and dissemination of curriculum for teachers to improve children's critical viewing skills and to teach nonviolent strategies for resolving conflicts

• development of resources to assist parents in the constructive and educational use of media with their children

During early childhood, the foundation is laid for future social, emotional, cognitive, and physical development. During this formative period, young children are particularly vulnerable to negative influences. In most instances, children have no control over the environmental messages they receive. Up until age seven or eight, children have great difficulty distinguishing fantasy from reality, and their ability to comprehend nuances of behavior, motivation, or moral complexity is limited. This special vulnerability of children necessitates increased vigilance to protect them from potentially negative influences. Parents are ultimately responsible for monitoring their children's viewing habits; however, parents cannot be omniscient and omnipresent in their children's lives. Parents need assistance in protecting their children from unhealthy exposure to violence. Therefore, limits must be placed on the content of programming directed at children. Restricting violence in children's programming should not be considered censorship, any more than is protecting children form exposure to pornography (Carlsson-Paige & Levin 1990). Likewise, industry standards to limit violence in children's programming should be developed as action taken in the public interest.

Rationale

This position statement is based on research examining the amount of violence present in the media as well as the effect of exposure to violent programming on children's development. Data clearly indicate that violence in the media has increased since 1980 and continues to increase. In addition, there is clear evidence to support the negative impact of viewing violence on children's development.

How violent are the media for children?

The problem of violence in the media is not new but has become much worse since the Federal Communication Commission's decision to deregulate children's commercial television in 1982. For example, air time for war cartoons jumped from 1½ hours per week in 1982 to 43 hours per week in 1986 (Carlsson-Paige & Levin 1987; Tuscherer 1988). Children's programs featured 18.6 violent acts per hour a decade ago and now have about 26.4 violent acts each hour (Gerbner 1990). Adults need to recognize that the content of programming has changed, and as a result the potential for negative effects on children's development is greater. Next to family, television and other media may be the most important sources of information for children, rivaling the school as a principal factor influencing their development.

How do violent media affect children's development?

Research consistently identifies three problems associated with heavy viewing of television violence: Children may become less sensitive to the pain and suffering of others; they may become more fearful of the world around them; and they may be more likely to behave in aggressive or harmful ways toward others (National Institute of Mental Health 1982; Singer & Singer 1984, 1986; Singer, Singer, & Rapaczynski 1984; Rule & Ferguson 1986; Simon 1989). Exposure to media violence leads children to see violence as a normal response to stress and as an acceptable means for resolving conflict.

Of great concern to early childhood educators is the negative effect of viewing violent programs on children's play. The importance of children's imaginative play to their cognitive and language development is well documented (Piaget 1962, 1963; Johnson, Christie, & Yawkey 1987). Research demonstrates that watching violent programs is related to less imaginative play and more imitative play in which the child simply mimics the aggressive acts observed on television (NIMH 1982). In addition, many media productions that regularly that regularly depict violence also promote program-based toys, which encourage children to imitate and reproduce in their play the actual behaviors seen on television or in movies. In these situations. children's creative and imaginative play is undermined, thus robbing children of the benefits of play for their development (Carlsson-Paige & Levin 1990). In their play, children imitate those characters reinforced for their aggressive behavior and rehearse the characters' scripts without creative or reflective thought. Children who repeatedly observe violent or aggressive problem-solving behavior in the media tend to rehearse what they see in their play and imitate those behaviors in real-life encounters (Huesmann 1986; Rule & Ferguson 1986; Eron & Huesmann 1987). In short, children who are frequent viewers of media violence learn that aggression is a successful and acceptable way to achieve goals and solve problems; they are less likely to benefit from creative, imaginative play as the natural means to express feelings, overcome anger, and gain self-control.

Recommendations

What should policymakers and broadcasters do?

NAEYC supports the reinstitution of FCC standards establishing limits on violent depictions during hours children are likely to watch television. Standards would also control the degree to which violence is depicted so as to be perceived by children as a normal and acceptable response to problems, as equated with power, as leading to reward or glorification of the perpetrator. An additional strategy would be to develop a parental guidance rating system for network and cable television, videotapes, and computer games similar to that established for movies.

NAEYC further supports the reestablishment of industry standards to limit children's exposure to violence. The self-regulating code of the National Association of Broadcasters (1980) was a responsible position of the television industry toward young children. As an immediate action, laws prohibiting the adoption of such voluntary standards as violations of anti-trust regulation should be repealed.

Industry standards should also limit advertising during children's programming in recognition of children's inability to distinguish the advertising from programming content and to prevent acts of aggression or violence being separated from consequences by intervening commercials. Studies show that children up to eight years of age are less likely to "learn the lesson" of a program when ads intervene between an anti-social act and its consequences.

Finally, broadcasting standards should prohibit product-based programming and feature-length programs whose primary purpose is to sell toys, especially when those toys facilitate imitation of violent or aggressive acts seen on television. Children are unable to evaluate the quality and play value of such products depicted on television. Program-based advertising creates in children an insatiable desire for these single-use toys; children start to believe that they can't play without the specific props seen on television (Carlsson-Paige & Levin 1990).

What can teachers do?

NAEYC believes that early childhood teachers have a responsibility to assist children in developing skills in nonviolent conflict resolution, to assist children to become critical viewers of all forms of media, and to encourage the constructive use of the media for instilling positive social values. Teachers need to be aware of what is currently being broadcast to children and to inform parents of the impact of violent media on children's development. Unfortunately, the effect of deregulation on the quality of children's television has made it necessary for teachers and parents to be more vigilant that they would have to be if the government and television industry acted more responsibly toward children.

Teachers can work with children when themes of television violence appear in their play to facilitate more appropriate problem solving and/or creative, imaginative play. Teachers should inform parents when negative or violent themes appear as a regular part of their children's play and support parents in their efforts to monitor children's viewing habits.

As professionals, early childhood educators should share their knowledge of child development and the effects of violent media viewing with legislators and sponsors of children's programming. It is the professional responsibility of early childhood educators to advocate for more developmentally and educationally appropriate programming for children. Teachers need to recognize that media are also a powerful teacher that can and should be used constructively with children. Contrary to popular belief, television viewing is not a passive activity; children are mentally active during television viewing (Anderson & Collins 1988). The use of media as an educational tool should not be rejected because much of commercial television currently lacks educational value or promotes violence. Instead, early childhood professionals should advocate for policy that eliminates violence and improves the educational value of media, and should use media constructively in their work with children.

What can parents do?

The absence of government regulation of children's television has made parents' job more difficult, necessitating more parental monitoring of what children see on television. This unfortunate situation places additional, unnecessary pressure on parents. Even when industry standards are developed, NAEYC believes that parents are responsible for monitoring the quality and quantity of the media to which their children are exposed. Standards will make the job easier, however. In the meantime, parents can watch television and other media with their children and evaluate the shows together. Children do not interpret programs the same way adults do. Adults need to talk with children about what they observe through the media, to find out how children are interpreting what they see and to help clarify misinterpretations. Parents can designate an approved list of media options for their children and give children choices from among approved shows.

Parents need to be aware that much of what children watch on television is not specifically intended for children. It has been estimated that only 10% of children's viewing time is spent watching children's television; the other 90% is spent watching programs designed for adults (Van Dyck 1983). Parents can assist children in finding alternatives to viewing adult television. In addition, parents can use videotapes of high quality children's programming and public television when commercial alternatives are not available. As consumers, parents should recognize and use their influence with sponsors of children's programs. The primary purpose of commercial television is not to entertain or to educate but to sell products. Parents can communicate with advertisers on programs that are valuable, as well as sponsors of programs that are violent. Parents can also help their children become educated consumers and involve them in writing complaints to broadcasters and companies that use violent images in an attempt to sell toys and other products. As taxpayers, parents can encourage their legislators to adopt policies to protect children from media violence.

Conclusion

The prevalence of violence in American society is a complex social problem that will not be easily solved. Violence in the media is only one manifestation of the larger society's fascination with violence. However, media violence is not just a reflection of violent society, it is also a contributor. If our nation wishes to produce future generations of productive adults who reject violence as a means of problem solving, we must reassert the vital role of government in protecting its most vulnerable citizens and, together, work to make media part of the solution.

References

Anderson, D., & P. Collins. 1988. *The impact on children's education: Television's influence on cognitive development.* Washington, DC: U.S. Department of Education, Office of Educational Research and Improvement.

Carlsson-Paige, N., & D. Levin. 1987. *The war play dilemma: Balancing needs and values in the early childhood classroom.* New York: Teachers College Press, Columbia University.

Carlsson-Paige, N., & D. Levin. 1990. *Who's calling the shots? How to respond effectively to children's fascination with war play and war toys.* Santa Cruz, CA: New Society.

Eron, L., & L. Huesmann. 1987. Television as a source of maltreatment of children. *School Psychology Review* 16: 195–202.

Gerbner, G., & N. Signorielli. 1990. *Violence profile 1967 through 1988–89: Enduring trends.* Philadelphia: University of Pennsylvania, Annenberg School of Communication.

Huesmann, L. 1986. Psychological processes promoting the relation between exposure to media violence and aggressive behavior by the viewer. *Journal of Social Issues* 42: 125–40.

Huston, A., B. Watkins, & D. Kunkel. 1989. Public policy and children's television. *American Psychologist* 44: 424–33.

Johnson, J., J. Christie, & T. Yawkey. 1987. *Play and early childhood development.* Glenview, IL: Scott, Foresman.

National Association of Broadcasters. 1980. *The television code* (21st ed). New York: Author.

National Institute of Mental Health. 1982. *Television and behavior: Ten years of scientific progress for the eighties. Vol 1: Summary report.* Washington, DC: U.S. Government Printing Office.

Piaget, J. 1962 [1951]. *Play, dreams, and imitation in children* (C. Gattegno & F.M. Hodgson, trans.). New York: Norton.

Piaget, J. 1963 [1936]. *The origins of intelligence in children.* (M. Cook, trans.). New York: Norton.

Rule, B., & T. Ferguson. 1986. The effects of media violence on attitudes, emotions and cognition. *Journal of Social Issues* 42: 29–50

Simon, P. 1989. Coming soon: An act that should reduce television violence. *Newsday* 21 August.

Singer, D., & J. Singer. 1984. TV violence: What's all the fuss about? *Television & Children* 7 (2): 30–41.

Singer, J.L., & D.G. Singer. 1986. Family experiences and television viewing as predictors of children's imagination, restlessness, and aggression. *Journal of Social Issues* 42: 107–24.

Singer, J., D. Singer, & W. Rapaczynski. 1984. *Journal of Communication* 34 (2): 73–89.

Tuscherer, P. 1988. *TV interactive toys: The new high tech threat to children.* Bend, OR: Pinnaroo.

Van Dyck, N.B. 1983. Families and television. *Television & Children* 6 (3): 3–11.

SAMPLE MATERIALS FROM A COMMUNITY ACTIVITY

Here are examples of the materials prepared for the Winnetka, Illinois, annual TV Tune-out week. The materials were used to help children, families, schools, and the whole community participate in and learn from the experience.

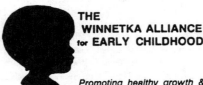

**THE
WINNETKA ALLIANCE
for EARLY CHILDHOOD**

Promoting healthy growth & development of children from birth to age eight

OVERVIEW OF THE 1997 TV TUNE OUT

The Winnetka Alliance for Early Childhood sponsored its **third annual community-wide TV Tune Out** from Thursday, Feb. 6 through Wednesday, Feb. 12. Children from approximately 3 to 10 years of age and their families were encouraged to turn off their televisions for seven days and, together, experience the adventure of a week with no television. Sixteen schools, including all public, private and parochial elementary schools, preschools and day care centers in Winnetka and Northfield were involved. Two preschools outside of Winnetka/Northfield, which enroll many children from those towns, also participated. **A total of 18 schools and over 4,000 children took part this year.**

The purpose of the TV Tune Out is not to suggest throwing out the family television set forever, nor is it to make families feel guilty about watching. Rather, it is to **help families get a better understanding of the role TV plays in their lives** and to explore other options.

During all three Tune Outs, many families discovered that TV influenced children's use of free time and also had an impact on their reading, playing, learning and in family interactions. Some liked how the removal of television enhanced the lives of family members. Parents reported more creative, involved play; better sibling relationships and interactive play; a quieter, more peaceful household (although some reported a louder, messier house!); more use of art materials, games and toys that had been unused or forgotten. A typical reaction: "I had no idea we used that TV so much!"

Many families made changes in their use of television, as a result of the Tune Out. A few families turned off the set and never turned it back on again. There were some who were reassured that they really didn't watch a lot of TV anyway. Others returned to their previous viewing habits as soon as the Tune Out ended. The Alliance encourages each family to use the TV Tune Out in whatever way suits it best.

The TV Tune Out fosters a wonderful **sense of community and a feeling that "we're all in this together."** To provide alternatives to television during the week, 36 merchants and organizations in Winnetka and Northfield sponsored events and activities. These were listed in the *TV Tune Out Guide*. There were a wide variety of activities available. For example, kids wearing TV Tune Out buttons could pick up a free pack of sports cards; see how color film is processed or how bagels are made; enjoy a TV Tune Out cookie or sundae; attend several story hours, a puppet show and a Hawaiian dance demonstration; and choose a grab bag prize. Also available were tours of Hadley School for the Blind and Dominick's Food Store; introductory Orff classes and concerts at the Music Center of the North Shore; an exhibit about trains at the Winnetka Historical Museum; and a Family TV Tune Out Party at the Kohl Children's Museum.

In response to suggestions from last year's evaluations, this year's schedule included several **community service opportunities.** Children could opt to participate in a nature conservation project or help clean up the Green Bay Trail or one of Winnetka's or Northfield's parks. Throughout the week, there were opportunities to cook for the homeless; prepare valentine baskets for the elderly; design centerpieces for a senior center; or make valentines for veterans.

Many schools held special events or celebrations during TV Tune Out Week. There were pajama parties and story hours at some of the preschools. Elementary schools held family fitness nights, spaghetti dinners, and created opportunities to play games instead of watch videos over the lunch hour. Many schools incorporated the Tune Out into their curriculum, asking children to chart activities they did instead of watching TV or keep journals throughout the week. It was a great opportunity for media education.

The theme of the 1997 TV Tune Out was to consider it **a week of exploration, not deprivation.** With the extra time gained from turning off the TV, children had time to discover new skills, hobbies and interests which they might choose to pursue afterwards.

Each TV Tune Out participant received a TV Tune Out button and a copy of the *TV Tune Out Guide,* which listed all activities, as well as ideas for projects and games to do at home. The Alliance was able to provide *Guides* and buttons to all, through the generosity of 21 community sponsors, who donated gifts that totaled over $5,000. Also available were several handouts and articles discussing the impact of television on children and families.

TV Tune Out Week was educational and enlightening. And it was fun, too.

THE WINNETKA ALLIANCE FOR EARLY CHILDHOOD

TV
TUNE OUT
FEBRUARY 1-7, 1996

TV TUNE OUT CONTRACT

We, the family of _____
(child's name)

hereby agree to the following terms and conditions:

    1. We will do our best not to view TV or engage in any TV-related activity such as playing video games, watching video tapes or taping TV shows for one week.

    2. We will make a positive effort to engage in other activities during the times that we might otherwise be watching TV.

    The period of this contract shall be from February 1, 1996 through February 7, 1996.

              Signed,

                        _____

                        _____

                        _____

                        _____

This contract is for you and your family. You do not need to return it.

What Did You Do During the Tune Out?
Families Share Their Successful Ideas

- "We built a fire in the fireplace every night."

- "We learned lots of new card games. Some are great for memorization and math skills. They also encourage interaction among siblings."

- "My children 'turned on' to the dress-up box during the Tune Out. We raided my closet and the attic to add several more pieces. The kids played with it all week."

- "We brought out the Legos--every set in the house--and another that we bought during the week. I was amazed at how engrossed the boys became."

- "We all felt that the house was too quiet with the TV silenced, so we played music all week. We even introduced some different kinds of music, including classical, jazz and Broadway shows."

- "We kept markers and paper next to the table. Before dinner, we would draw, color or play word games. My kids still do this between the hours of 5:00 and 6:00 p.m."

- "We pulled out board games that had been shelved for years. One Monopoly® game went on for days."

- "We pulled out old photo albums and put together new ones."

- "We put a magnetic poetry board in the den and we worked on it as a family. We kept building on what had been written."

- "We took long walks after dinner."

- "We took lots of trips to the library and the bookstore."

- We set up a card table with a jigsaw puzzle and we kept it up all week. Family members would return to it again and again to put in a piece or two."

- "One night we taught the kids to do the Twist, the Mashed Potato, the Bunny Hop and other silly dances from our past. We laughed so hard! Then we took videos of ourselves (but didn't watch them till the Tune Out was over!)"

- "We made collages from catalogs left over from the holidays. Sometimes we made "theme" collages (like sports, red things, food, babies)."

- "We got some huge cardboard boxes and the kids made them into forts, houses, etc. and used them all week long."

- "We gathered in front of the fireplace (which we actually lit several times) and read a chapter from a book aloud each night before bed. My kids can't wait for the Tune Out to start again, so we can do it again."

SAMPLE FLYER FROM A LOCAL EVENT

This flyer describes a Toy Gun Trade-in that was sponsored by the Lion and Lamb Project. It is the kind of event that can be organized by local groups.

Violent Toy Trade-In
The Lion & Lamb Project

Magicians

Craft Activities

Clowns

Musicians

Old-Fashioned Games

Door Prizes

What: Bring in violent toys such as Super Squirters, toy guns, Power Rangers, Ninja Turtles, and video cartridges from violent Nintendo and Sega games and help turn them into a Peace Sculpture. Children who bring in violent toys will receive discount coupons for creative, nonviolent children's merchandise. (Children who don't own violent toys can bring a list of their favorite nonviolent toys and receive the same coupon.)

When: Saturday, December 2, 12:30 - 3:30 p.m.

Where: Rolling Terrace Elementary School, 705 Bayfield Street, Takoma Park, Maryland

Who: Children 5 and older are invited

Why: If you believe glorified violence is not an appropriate form of entertainment for our children, come join us for an afternoon of alternative play!

How: **From the District,** take 13th Street north toward Takoma Park (the street name changes to Piney Branch Avenue.) Continue on Piney Branch until you pass Flower Avenue. At the second light after Flower Avenue, turn right on Barron Street. The school is straight ahead at the intersection with Bayfield Street.

From the Beltway, take University Boulevard exit toward Langley Park. After one mile, make a right at the light onto Piney Branch Avenue. At the first light, turn left on Barron Street. The school is straight ahead.

READER FEEDBACK

Please take a few minutes to share your efforts to combat the hazards of media culture. Copy this form and use the space below to tell me about how you use and build on the action ideas suggested in *Remote Control Childhood?* Describe your experiences with and ideas about action steps not included here. The information you share will be used to expand our understanding about how to responsibly and effectively deal with the media culture in children's lives.

Thanks for sharing this information with me.

—D.L.

Send completed forms to:
Diane Levin, Wheelock College, 200 The Riverway, Boston, MA 02215.
Or e-mail them to:
dlevin@wheelock.edu

Information about NAEYC

NAEYC is . . .

. . . a membership-supported organization of people committed to fostering the growth and development of children from birth through age 8. Membership is open to all who share a desire to serve and act on behalf of the needs and rights of young children.

NAEYC provides . . .

. . . educational services and resources to adults who work with and for children, including

- *Young Children,* the journal for early childhood educators
- **books, posters, brochures,** and **videos** to expand your knowledge and commitment to young children, with topics including infants, curriculum, research, discipline, teacher education, and parent involvement
- an **Annual Conference** that brings people together from all over the country to share their expertise and advocate on behalf of children and families
- **Week of the Young Child** celebrations sponsored by NAEYC Affiliate Groups across the nation to call public attention to the needs and rights of children and families
- **insurance plans** for individuals and programs
- **public affairs** information and access to information available through NAEYC resources and communication systems for knowledgeable advocacy efforts at all levels of government and through the media
- the **National Academy of Early Childhood Programs,** a voluntary accreditation system for high-quality programs for children
- the **National Institute for Early Childhood Professional Development,** which offers resources and services to improve professional preparation and development of early childhood educators
- **Young Children International** to promote international communication and information exchanges

For free information about membership, publications, or other NAEYC services, visit the **NAEYC Website** at **http://www.naeyc.org/naeyc.**

National Association for the Education of Young Children
1509 16th Street, NW
Washington, DC 20036-1426
800-424-2460 or 202-232-8777